Photographs by Edward Vebell
Drawings by Dick Kohfield

The Dial Press
New York 1976

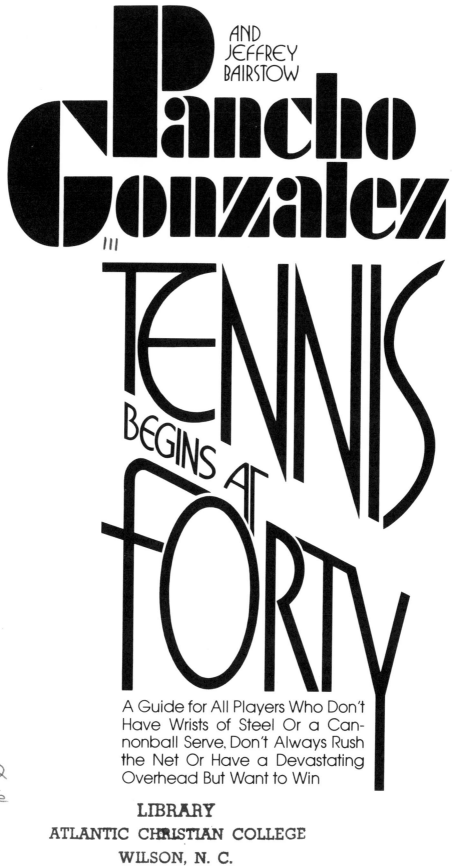

Pancho Gonzalez

AND JEFFREY BAIRSTOW

TENNIS BEGINS AT FORTY

A Guide for All Players Who Don't Have Wrists of Steel Or a Cannonball Serve, Don't Always Rush the Net Or Have a Devastating Overhead But Want to Win

Manufactured in the United States of America

First printing   1976

Designed by James L. McGuire

Library of Congress Cataloging in Publication Data

Gonzalez, Pancho, 1928–
Tennis begins at forty.
1. Tennis. I. Bairstow, Jeffrey, 1939–
joint author. II. Title.
GV995.G63   796.34'22   76-9416
ISBN 0-8037-5945-2

CONTENTS

81-   C13

CONTENTS

TENNIS
BEGINS AT
FORTY

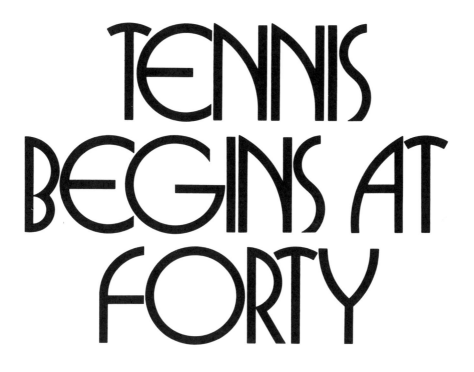

TENNIS BEGINS AT FORTY

TENNIS BEGINS AT FORTY

I can hear you saying, "What on earth does he mean? How can a guy who has played championship tennis all his life suggest that tennis begins at forty?" Well, take that forty as more of a symbol than a specific age. Tennis is a sport that anyone can learn but unlike, say, basketball, you do not have to start at an early age. In fact, the recent boom in the popularity of tennis offers proof that many new players have started the game in their thirties, forties, fifties, and even older. It is for tennis players of these ages that this book is written—for those new to the sport, for those who haven't played tennis in years, for those who play regularly and well but no longer can rush the net with their accustomed regularity for that game-winning point.

So, what I am trying to do is to show you how adult players can develop a game that will give them satisfaction no matter what their age and ability level, and how they can enjoy tennis not merely into their forties, but, as the U.S. Tennis Association so rightly claims, as a lifetime sport. Take that forty as a symbol for the adult player and you'll understand the reason for this instruction book.

Having passed the age of forty a few years ago I have seen a few changes in my game and in my attitudes toward the sport. Naturally, I've had to make some adjustments in my tactics and style of play, but I'm finding that I enjoy tennis even more now that some of the pressure is gone. No longer do I have to submit to punishing daily workouts to prepare myself for the rigors of the tournament circuit or the grind of the one-night stands that were the norm for professional matches when I first signed as a pro. Of course, I do keep myself fit—and that's a must for the older player—and I do play competitively in the national senior championships. But I'm no longer in the pressure cooker of international competition, and that has helped me realize that a different kind of tennis is played by the intermediate adult player.

TENNIS BEGINS AT FORTY

Since I can't cover the court as fast as I used to, I've been playing a lot more doubles, especially with Hugh Stewart, one of the world's top-ranked senior players who is now on my staff at Caesars Palace in Las Vegas. Hugh and I still have the ball control we had in our younger days, even though we may not hit the ball quite as hard as we used to.

This book will show you some of the secrets of stroking that I hope will help you develop the ball control that's essential for the better intermediate player's game. You'll also see how to put that kind of strokemaking to work in both doubles and singles play. Although I feel that the older player will often find doubles an especially enjoyable game, increasing age doesn't mean that you will have to give up singles entirely. At forty-six, I won the senior (over-forty-five) singles title at Forest Hills and I intend to continue to enter major senior singles events as long as the competition makes it fun to play.

As a matter of fact, when you've had a chance to digest some of the material in this book I think you'll learn even more about stroking and tactics for the older player if you go to Forest Hills or any major tournament with a seniors' contest and watch the former great players who are still competing as strongly as ever. As an adult player you'll do well to emulate such senior players as Frank Sedgman, Vic Seixas, Pancho Segura, even Bobby Riggs, and, of course, myself. All those former champions still play an excellent game of tennis. Their speed and reflexes may be a little slower, but they can make up for that by being even more accurate than they used to be and by being a little more crafty.

And that's where the older player can really come on strong. When you're young, you can blast away at the ball with cannonball serves, hard-hit drives, and powerful volleys. Such a game can often blow your opponent right off the court. I'll admit to having done that more than a few times in my youth. However, as you get older, you rely less on your muscles and

more on brain power. You use more deception on your shots so that your opponent has a harder time figuring out where you're going to place your next shot. That fraction of a second gained means your opponent will have less time to prepare a return. Make percentage play the key to your game. By that I mean don't always try for a winner but make sure you get the ball back so you can stay in the point.

Consistency, of course, should be the hallmark of the mature player's game. Your strokes should be so well grooved that shotmaking is instinctive. Your placements should always have a good margin of safety. If you can be consistent in returning the ball, your opponent will almost certainly make enough errors to give you the match. If you go for winners all the time, you may end up making so many errors you lose the match. If you don't believe me, try scoring the winners and errors during a seniors' match. I'm pretty sure you'll find the winner of the match will have made far fewer errors than the loser.

Unfortunately, consistency can be obtained in only one way—by lots of practice. I'll be saying this several times in this book but there is no substitute for daily practice. Even if you can afford only 15 or 20 minutes a day, your game will benefit more from a few minutes of concentrated practice than from three or four times as much match play. Whether you have been playing tennis for ten years or ten days you can always use some more practice. If you can't find a court or a practice partner, put a rebound net or a backboard up in your back yard and hit a few balls every day.

An equally important objective for the older player is to keep physically fit. A daily tennis practice session plus a few weekend or evening matches will not be enough to keep your body in top physical condition. With the approval of your physician you should also work at a physical training program designed for your age and life style. In Chapter 11 I make some suggestions for exercises to help your conditioning and stamina. Have a physical training expert set up a program for you and stick to it. Many YMCAs have early morning or evening conditioning programs for desk-bound people. Try one of those if you don't have the willpower to carry out a program by yourself.

Even with a proper conditioning program, you won't have the stamina of a much younger player and you should alter your game accordingly. When I was playing in international championships and was in top condition, I always conserved my energy before a big match—even to the point of refusing to sign autographs. Not only should you conserve your energy before playing tennis, you should also eliminate waste motion and take frequent breathers during a match. For example, I now bounce the ball before I serve because that gives me a slight breathing space and time to collect my thoughts to concentrate on the serve.

You'll also have to appreciate your limits. If the day is so hot and humid that you begin to feel lightheaded or your vision becomes blurry after an hour or two of play, make your apologies and stop playing. Get some rest and you'll soon revive to play another day. I've always believed in a shower and complete rest after a tiring match. As I get older the value of a rest after a match increases greatly. An hour's sleep lets the body recover naturally and leaves you with a feeling of well-being after physical activity.

All this may sound like pretty grave advice but I make no apology for it. If you want to play tennis well, and I'm assuming that you do since you're reading this book, you'll have to devote some pretty serious effort to the sport. But I think you'll find that the benefits more than justify the effort.

If tennis begins at thirty or forty or older for you, I'm sure you'll soon discover that tennis is truly a family sport. You can play with your spouse or with your children and still have lots

of fun even if your ability levels are quite different. I enjoy playing with my wife and children, even though I sometimes feel that they don't quite devote the effort to practice that I'd like to see! My eldest son, Richard, and I have won a couple of national father-and-son doubles titles. It's quite a thrill for all the family when two members win a competition like that.

I think you'll also find that once tennis has begun for you, it won't stop. The U.S. Tennis Association issues national rankings for players in the seventy-five-and-older age category. And those rankings are for both singles and doubles play. Not only do those seventy year olds enjoy playing tennis, they also get a huge kick out of beating each other and younger players, too! I fully expect to continue playing tennis for the rest of my life. I hope this book will help you to do the same.

2

THE
GROUND
STROKES

THE GROUND STROKES

Whether you are over or under forty, male or female, a social or a professional tennis player, the framework on which your game is built will depend on your ground strokes—especially your forehand and backhand drives. Many of the principles of the basic ground strokes, of course, apply to other tennis strokes. If you can get the execution of your ground strokes grooved, these patterns will come naturally when you progress to the other strokes.

Probably the most frequently repeated tennis instruction is: "Keep your eye on the ball." All too often it is ignored. The result is either missing the shot completely or hitting the ball away from the center of your racket. To prevent those errors, try to watch the ball actually hit the strings of your racket during practice sessions. Look at the ball as though you expect it to disappear at any moment. Keep your eyes fixed on the ball throughout the stroke. As you get older and your eyesight weakens, you will have to concentrate even harder on watching the ball.

An instruction not as frequently heard, but equally important, is: "Move your weight forward." If you always transfer your weight from your back foot to your front foot as you hit the ball, you'll feel a tremendous increase in the power of the shot. You don't have to be big and heavy to hit a tennis ball with power. Just watch Ken Rosewall, one of the smallest players in top-flight competition. Rosewall doesn't swing hard but he puts all his weight into the shot with the result that his ground strokes have more pace, speed, and momentum than those of players who are much larger. Over-forty players may lack muscle flexibility but their strokes don't have to lack power if they learn to step into the shot so that they are moving forward automatically as they begin to swing toward the ball.

Although tennis is only a game, the object is to win and you can do so only when concentrating. The older you become the more important it is to concentrate solely on the game. When on the tennis court, shut out any problems that have been on your mind during the day. Concentrate on each point as you play it. Forget the mistake you just made or the poor line call made by your opponent. Even a pro's concentration is often destroyed by a disputed line call.

Whenever your game seems to be falling apart, remember the three instructions I've just emphasized. Make a conscious effort to put the missing principles back in action and, chances are, you'll soon see an improvement.

THE GRIPS

How you grip a tennis racket is largely a matter of personal preference. You'll see that the top players use a variety of grips, but they have such natural stroking ability they can use grips that might be awkward for the average player. Because the grip is important for the beginning player, I usually suggest players start with separate forehand and backhand grips and then, as their games improve, modify those grips until one grip is used for all strokes.

If you have been playing the sport for several years and your stroking is adequate, I'd suggest you stick with the grip you now use. If you are a beginner you should use the conventional forehand grip, sometimes called the "Eastern" forehand or the "shake-hands grip," and switch to the Eastern backhand grip for your backhand strokes.

You can get a proper Eastern forehand grip by cradling the throat of your racket in your non-racket hand and shaking hands with the racket. Your fingers should wrap around the

THE METHOD FOR OBTAINING THE GRIP

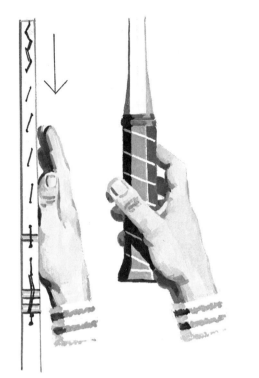

racket quite naturally and be slightly apart. Alternatively, you can place the palm of your racket hand against the strings and move it down the shaft until you can grip the handle by closing your fingers around it. Hold the racket firmly so that it cannot be pulled out of your hand by a friend. Don't try to squeeze it so hard that your wrist muscles tire quickly.

To get the correct Eastern backhand grip, start from the forehand grip and rotate your hand about a quarter of a turn over the top of the racket handle. In this position, the "V" between your thumb and forefinger will be slightly to the left of the racket handle. Keep your fingers spread apart a little and grip the racket firmly. I recommend that you use the backhand grip for your serve and volleys in addition to your backhand ground strokes.

THE EASTERN FOREHAND GRIP

THE EASTERN BACKHAND GRIP

THE CONTINENTAL GRIP

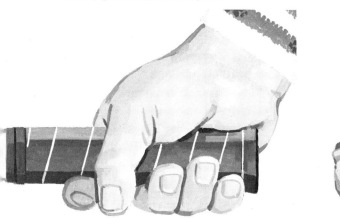

THE GROUND STROKES

As your game improves you may find that your forehand and backhand grips come closer together until you develop one grip for all your strokes. This multi-purpose grip is sometimes called the "Continental" grip since it was first used by several European players. The Continental grip is generally closer to the Eastern backhand than to the forehand. The heel of your hand will be almost on top of the racket with the "V" of your forefinger and thumb very slightly to the left of the top of the racket.

You'll have to be fairly strong to use the Continental grip effectively because your arm will not be directly behind the racket as it is with the Eastern grips. However, if you play a fast net game I'd suggest you try to use one grip for all your strokes—either the Continental or the Eastern backhand.

Some top players, especially those like Bjørn Borg and Rod Laver with wristy topspin strokes, have grips that might once have been called "Western" because they were favored by players from California. However, the Western grips are too hard for the average player to master and so don't offer any particular advantage.

If you have any doubts about the effectiveness of your grip, consult an expert—your local teaching pro. Chances are he'll recommend that you stay with your current grip. If he does suggest a change, be prepared to devote lots of effort to mastering the new grip—the results should be worth it.

THE READY POSITION

THE READY POSITION

When you are waiting to hit a ground stroke you should stand a foot or so behind the baseline just to the rear of the center mark. Bend your knees slightly and keep your weight entirely on the balls of your feet. You should be crouched like a cat, ready to move rapidly in any direction. Hold your racket straight out in front of you with the head above your wrist.

15

Try to anticipate your opponent's shot and make your move as soon as the ball comes off your opponent's racket. You can improve your anticipation by learning what return is most likely. For example, if you hit a shot to your right, your opponent will, most likely, return the ball crosscourt to your left. You should be poised to move to the left. But don't move before the other player hits the ball, because on detecting your move, your opponent will hit the ball behind you and catch you on the wrong foot.

After you have analyzed the direction of your opponent's shot, get into position as quickly as possible so you can be set before hitting the ball. When you have completed your stroke, return to the center of the court just behind the baseline and take up the ready position for the next shot.

THE FOREHAND

Virtually every beginner starts playing tennis by hitting forehands. The stroke is relatively easy and it quickly becomes one of the stronger shots for most intermediate players. Yet the forehand can easily become an inconsistent shot because as you develop too much confidence, your swing shortens and you take your eyes off the ball. So, it's important to work on your forehand even when you feel it is already a good strong shot for you. Never neglect to practice your strengths.

Although many over-forty players have a passable forehand, their shots do not have the consistent depth of professionals like Jimmy Connors and Chris Evert. That's mainly because the average player doesn't transfer body weight when making contact with the ball and put the necessary weight into the shot. Often, I invite guests to hit a few balls with me, and at first they're so nervous, or so intimidated, they can scarcely swing at the ball. When they do get a ball over the net, it barely manages to reach the service line. At that point, I tell them to try to hit the ball over the back fence. Then, they put some weight into the shot and hit harder. Much to their surprise the ball rarely reaches the back fence, but instead they find their shots going to the baseline. When you can hit a forehand well, go for depth and you'll have a drive that will keep your opponent on the baseline.

Intermediate players often stand in a poor position when hitting forehands. Instead of turning sideways to the net in a closed stance, they face the net in an open stance. As you prepare to hit a forehand, step forward and around with your left foot (if you are right-handed) so that it is in front of you as you hit and you are completely sideways to the net. This is the only position in which you can get the proper weight transfer.

You should always have a mental picture of the stroke you wish to hit. When you have studied the accompanying high-speed photo sequences, you may find that practice in front of a mirror will help groove your shots. Try to put that picture into your strokes as you practice and eventually you'll find stroking becomes instinctive.

1   2   3   4

HOW TO HIT A FOREHAND

Almost all your forehand drives will be hit from behind the baseline so you should take a ready position a few feet behind the baseline close to the center mark (see page 15). As soon as you realize your opponent is hitting a shot to your forehand, turn your body sideways to the net (frames 1, 2). This produces two important results. First, it starts your racket back early (3). Second, it positions you to run a few steps to reach the ball, if necessary.

1   2   3   4

THE FOREHAND DRIVE Front View

6   7   8

Take your racket back as quickly as you can until it is pointing to the back fence (4, 5). I use a looping backswing, but that is largely a matter of personal preference. You may find a level straight backswing is easier. How you get the racket back is not as important as getting it back early.

When your racket is back, your weight will be almost entirely on your back foot and your body still sideways to the net. As you start your forward swing, transfer your weight to your forward foot (6) so that your body weight is behind the shot. Proper weight transfer will put power into the shot and help you get depth.

6   7   8

9   10   11   12

The forward swing of the forehand is a whiplike action in which the racket follows the forearm in the early part of the motion (7) and then speeds up as you hit through the ball. This whiplike action is created by bringing your shoulder and arm around in a smooth arc (8). Keep your wrist firm and resist the temptation to flick at the ball. Only if you have the wrist muscles of a Rod Laver can you do so effectively.

You should make contact with the ball at the approximate center of the 180-degree arc of your swing. Contact should be at a point about waist level, just in front of your forward hip. If the ball is low, bend your knees to get the plane of the

9   10   11   12

THE FOREHAND DRIVE Front View (continued)

racket's swing down to the flight of the ball. As you make contact, your weight should be completely on your front foot, and only the toes of your rear foot should still be in contact with the ground.

Hit the ball flat with the racket face near vertical, keeping the ball on the racket for as long as possible. You should have the feeling that you are lifting the ball slightly to get it over the net (9). If you were to hit the ball without the slight lift, it would, of course, go straight into the net. This lifting action, caused by the slight upward motion of the racket as you hit and continue into the follow-through, will often put a little natural topspin on the ball, causing it to drop a little faster in the other court.

I don't advocate the use of heavy topspin for intermediate players, but you will find a topspin shot is easier on the forehand than on the backhand. On the forehand, your hand is gripping the racket from behind so that you can not only use a lifting action but also roll the racket over a little for extra spin. But don't try that until your forehand is really grooved.

After you hit the ball, don't slow your stroke. Let the racket follow through naturally (10) until it finishes across your body on the opposite side (11). At the completion of the shot you should be looking over your stroking arm (12), with your weight shifted so completely that your back foot is swinging forward. Now you should return to the center of the baseline and get into the ready position for the next shot.

When practicing the forehand, always aim your shots. While the stroke is always the same whether you are hitting crosscourt or down the line, you can get direction by changing the timing of your hit. Simply hit a little later in the ball's flight for down the line and a little earlier for crosscourt. Put tennis ball cans on the opposing court and see if you can hit them as you practice.

THE
GROUND
STROKES

THE FOUR MOST COMMON FOREHAND ERRORS

Your greatest fault is not watching the ball. This is particularly true on the forehand, where competent players will develop so much confidence that they feel they can hit the shot with their eyes closed. You can't. Watch the ball, not your opponent, right up to the point of contact if you can. There is a physical problem in hitting a forehand because most of us sight a ball with our right eye—the one that is farther away from the on-coming ball when hitting forehand. So it's easy for the left eye to become distracted by an opponent's move. Forget your opponent until you've hit the ball.

The second common fault is not turning sideways to the net. To hit an effective forehand and transfer your weight correctly, you must turn your body sideways to the net by stepping out with your opposite foot. Get that foot around so that your stance is really closed. When I was a young player I used to exaggerate the forward step so that when I played in a match that forward step was instinctive. You should practice stepping and hitting until it becomes an instinctive reaction.

The third forehand problem afflicts both professionals and amateurs—not taking a full swing at the ball. The arc of the forehand should be a full 180 degrees from the end of the backswing to the follow-through out in front. If you are going to hit forehands that strike your opponent's baseline, you must have a full backswing and a complete forward swing with an uninterrupted follow-through. An abbreviated swing will result in a short shot, allowing your opponent to come in and either hit a winner or go for the net, where he will be in a commanding position.

Finally, many players suffer from overconfidence about their forehand. How many times have you hit excellent forehands during practice or pre-match warm-up and then been unable to hit the same forehands in the match? It's all too easy to become overconfident and forget the basic principles of watching the ball, preparing early, turning sideways to the net, hitting through the ball, and finishing with a full follow-through. If your forehand suddenly falls apart, go over the basics again and go out and practice until that familiar feeling comes back.

Forehand Checklist

1. Get your racket back as soon as possible and make sure that it continues back until it is perpendicular to the rear fence.
2. Bend your knees so that your swing gets down to the level of the ball. Your waist should be almost level with the ball's flight.
3. Step out in front with your opposite foot to bring your body sideways to the net. Transfer your weight onto that forward foot as you hit through the ball.
4. Hit the ball just ahead of your forward hip or even earlier if you can manage it.

THE BACKHAND

Although many beginners think the backhand is a difficult stroke, it is actually a more natural stroke than the forehand. As you hit a forehand your arm has to cross in front of your body, which produces a cramping action in the follow-through. By contrast, the backhand is made with a swing away from the body, free of restriction in arm movement. Also, you have to pivot your body to begin the backswing for the backhand so that you automatically adopt the proper side-to-the-net stance. Many right-handed players are faster taking off toward the left because they are naturally right-footed and can make a quicker start off the stronger right foot. So why do players have problems with the backhand?

There are probably two reasons, and most intermediate players seem to suffer from both faults. First, few players practice the backhand as much as the forehand. Watch the players on your local courts as they warm up. They will probably hit two or three times as many forehands as backhands. While you should never neglect to practice your strengths, it is equally essential that you practice to improve your weak shots. If your backhand is weak, practice it for 15 minutes each time you go out on a court. You'll soon see improvement.

The second problem is that the backhand is hit with the forearm and wrist ahead of the racket. This tends to make the backhand a weak and wristy shot unless you remember to keep a very firm wrist. The pros, like Rod Laver, Arthur Ashe, and myself, can hit a good backhand with a wristy action but it's not something I'd suggest for the average player. Hit with a firm wrist and forearm and you'll be surprised at the power your backhand will suddenly develop. Of course, you must have your body behind the shot to get maximum power.

When you've gotten a mental image of the stroke by imitating the photo sequence in front of a mirror, go out and practice your backhand. Not just a few shots, but 15 minutes or longer at a time. And keep at it until you no longer have to apologize for your backhand.

THE BACKHAND DRIVE Side View

1   2   3   4

HOW TO HIT A BACKHAND

As soon as you see your opponent hit the ball and you realize that it will be coming on your backhand side, start to get into position for your return. From the basic ready position (see page 15), pivot the upper half of your body (frame 1) so that you are sideways to the net, ready either to run into the proper position or to continue with your backswing if the ball is coming relatively close to you.

Take the racket back as quickly (2) and as smoothly as you can, using your other hand to guide it. Whether you take the

1   2   3   4

THE BACKHAND DRIVE Front View

5   6   7   8

racket back with a slight looping action (3, 4), as I am doing in the photo sequences on these pages, or in a straight line is not really very important. However, do get it all the way back (5) so you can make a full forward swing. Your racket should be so far back that you can only just see it out of the corner of your left eye (6). Don't watch the racket, though: keep your eye on the ball.

As you complete the backswing, bring your forward foot around in front of you and step toward the ball, keeping your weight on your back foot until you start your forward swing. As you swing forward (7), try to meet the ball so that its flight and the center of your racket are on the same plane (8). That

6   7   8

9   10   11   12

way you'll be hitting through the ball, which helps you keep it on the racket as long as possible and allows you to control its direction.

Make contact with the ball just ahead of your forward hip (9) and push the racket out in the direction that you want the ball to go (10). Top professional players will hit the ball even farther out front but that's not something I'd recommend for intermediate players—it's harder to control the ball when it's that far away from you.

As you hit the ball you should be transferring your weight forward to put power into the shot. At the point of contact, all your weight should be on your front foot. If you were to stop

9   10   11   12

THE BACKHAND DRIVE Front View (continued)

me as I hit my backhand, you'd find that I could stand on my front foot—I have so little weight on the back one. Weight transfer is one of the major differences between the weekend and the professional tennis player. A pro can hit a ball at 50 or 60 percent of his maximum strength and still have more power than a good club player. The pro puts total body weight into the shot by moving forward as the ball is hit.

If you are moving forward as you hit the ball, you'll find the follow-through comes naturally (11)—you can't stop the racket in mid-stroke. Follow through out in front in the direction you want the ball to go. Let your arm complete the arc of the swing so that your racket ends up high on the same side of your body (12). You can now bring your back foot forward for balance and return your racket to the ready position for the next shot. If you had to move away from the center of the baseline to hit the backhand, then sidestep quickly back to that spot, keeping your eyes on the ball and anticipating your next move.

THE GROUND STROKES

THE FOUR MOST COMMON BACKHAND ERRORS

Probably you have many times seen a player hit a backhand shot that loops high over the net or is so weak that it doesn't even get over the net. That player is usually committing *the most common error—not putting body weight into the shot—* and is, in fact, falling away from the ball by letting the weight remain on the rear foot. The cure for this problem is to go out and practice backhands with your weight moving onto your front foot. Make the opposite baseline your target—not the net. If you aim for the baseline you'll have to put your weight into the shot.

The second most common backhand fault is not watching the ball. If a player is watching the opponent out of the corner of one eye, a slight movement by that opponent will be enough to take the player's attention off the ball, resulting in a muffed shot. Some players look toward the place where they want to hit the ball. Even I am guilty of taking my eyes off the ball from time to time. If you can, have someone take video-tape or movie film of you hitting the ball. If the film shows that you are not watching the ball, concentrate on the ball's flight. Watch the ball as close to the racket as you can. Practice is the only cure for this fault.

The third major fault is not getting down to the level of the ball. You will make an effective hit only if you keep the racket head up so that the shaft is about parallel with the ground as you make contact with the ball. You should hit a ground stroke at about waist level. If the ball is low, bending your knees will take your waist down to the level of the ball. It will also bring your eyes closer to the ball so that you can see it better.

The fourth common problem with the backhand of interme-diate players is holding the racket too loosely, resulting in little or no control over the direction of shots. You should hold your racket so firmly that it cannot be pulled out of your grasp by another person. However, don't hold it in a rigid grip. When you hit the ball, tighten your grip a little more so that your wrist will also tighten up automatically. I recommend that you put your thumb behind the racket handle for extra support. And, of course, you can strengthen your grip any time by squeezing an old tennis ball.

Backhand Checklist

1. Pivot your body so you are sideways to the net with your racket back so far that it is perpendicular to the net.
2. Transfer your weight forward as you hit so that all your body weight is on your front foot when you contact the ball.
3. Use a firm grip, and tighten it just before you hit the ball.
4. Don't stop your forward motion after the hit. Follow through out in front and let your rear foot come through as you complete the stroke.

THE SERVE AND RETURN OF SERVE

THE SERVE AND RETURN OF SERVE

The serve is the most critical part of any player's game. This stroke provides the one opportunity to control everything—the position of the ball, the timing of the shot, the position of your body, and so on. If you can get it all together for your serve, then you stand a very good chance of winning the point outright. On the other hand, if your serve is off then you will, most likely, give the point to your opponent by double faulting or hitting such a weak serve that the other player can hit a winning return. Of course, there's nothing in tennis as satisfying as hitting a booming cannonball serve that flashes past your opponent for an ace—a winning serve that the other player can't even get a racket on. Far too many social tennis players like to show off by blasting away at their first serves. Inevitably, the majority of those show-off serves go out and the second serve that follows is a weak, played-for-safety pooping shot that the other player can rightly slam away for a winner.

Many intermediate players just don't realize that you are only as good as your second serve—a shot that you must get in to avoid double faulting and yet a shot that must have enough pace and spin to be difficult for your opponent to return. So I think *it's very important for the intermediate player, and especially the older player who may not have the muscular strength for a booming flat serve, to develop a consistent second serve.* If you have a good second serve that you don't have to worry about, your first attempt will be more relaxed and you'll automatically develop a tougher first serve.

I emphasize the slice serve for the intermediate player. This serve has a combination of sidespin and topspin that will make the ball clear the net by at least a couple of feet and yet still curve down into the court with a good margin of safety. As the ball hits, it will, on most relatively fast surfaces, skid and veer off to one side, which will give the receiver a few problems in guessing its exact direction after the bounce.

34

THE SERVE AND RETURN OF SERVE

If you have a good slice serve, there's no reason you shouldn't use it for both your first and second serves. But you'll win more points with the shot if you have a variety of serves and can vary the pace and spin on each one. By mixing up your serves, you'll keep the receiver guessing, and the returns will be less effective if the other player has trouble diagnosing your serve. So, once you've found a reliable slice serve, I think you should experiment with the flat serve (especially if you're tall and have a powerful swing) and, later, with the topspin or American twist serve. A flat serve is useful when you want to go for an ace on your first serve, and the topspin serve is good as an alternative to the slice for a second serve. The topspin serve kicks away sharply as it bounces, so it's a very difficult serve to return.

There's no excuse for a poor serve—serving well is simply a matter of practice. When I see club players practicing, they hit ground strokes for several minutes and usually end the practice session with no more than half a dozen serves. Then the players begin a set by allowing any number of serves until the first one goes in. Nothing could be worse. If you're going to play a set, abide by the rules from the very beginning. If your serve is weak, it's the one shot you can practice by yourself—in your own back yard if necessary. Get a bucket of balls and practice your serve for 20 minutes every day until you know what you can and can't do with it. But when you practice, remember you're practicing your second serve—all your practice serves should go in.

Many intermediate players have serves that lack consistency—not because they can't hit the ball, but because they don't consistently place the ball in the right place to hit it effectively. Probably the most significant key to the serve is a good ball toss; that's why I'm devoting the next section of this chapter to a lesson on the placement of the ball for the serve. So, even before you take your bucket of balls out to hit some

serves, practice the toss without hitting the ball. If you can, find a room in your house where the ceiling is a few inches higher than the highest point you can reach with your racket. Stick a piece of tape on the ceiling and practice tossing the ball so that it barely touches that mark. Or hang a tin can from the rafters of your garage and practice tossing so that you barely disturb the suspended can.

Some weekend players never hit an effective slice serve because they use the wrong grip. If, like most players, you begin tennis by learning how to hit forehands, you may have a tendency to adopt the forehand grip for the serve. Nothing could be more wrong. The only serve you'll be able to hit with that grip is a flat serve, and not a very good one at that. *I recommend a backhand grip for all your serves, but especially for the slice serve.* If you find the backhand grip awkward at first, just keep trying until you have a grip with the palm of your hand on top of the handle. That grip will help you get the wrist snap essential for an effective serve.

An advantage of using one grip for all your serves is that your stroke will be disguised until the very last moment before the hit. That way your opponent won't be able to read your serve until after the ball has left your racket, which will allow less time to prepare for the return. *I think disguise is an important part of the serve for any player, but it's especially important for older players who want to gain every ounce of advantage from the one shot that is completely under their control.*

THE BALL TOSS Side View

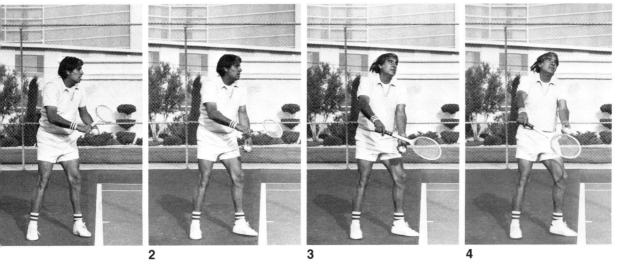

2   3   4

THE BALL TOSS

The ball toss is probably the most critical part of your service action. Once you have a consistent toss you'll be able to hit the ball in the same place each time. So it's just as important to work on your toss as it is to work on the hitting part of the serve.

To place the ball, start by holding it in the tips of your fingers (frame 1). Your hold on the ball should be so slight

2   3   4

THE BALL TOSS Front View

THE BALL TOSS Side View (continued)

5   6   7   8

that another player could lift the ball out of your hand very easily. Stand in a comfortable position sideways to the net with your body relaxed and your knees slightly bent. Drop your ball hand to your side (2, 3) and bring it up again, with your arm outstretched, in a smooth, continuous arc (4, 5, 6). When your arm is about level with the top of your head (7), gently open your fingers so that the ball is released into the air (8) and can continue upward (9, 10). On a very good toss there will be so little finger and wrist action that the ball will barely spin as it goes up in the air. The ball should go a few inches higher than your maximum reach (9, 10, 11, 12).

5   6   7   8

THE BALL TOSS Front View (continued)

If your placement in the air is correct, the ball will fall a few inches to the right of and about a foot in front of your forward foot. If you were to let the ball drop without hitting it, it should land within a few inches of the same spot each time. In fact, when you practice the toss, it's a good idea to place a bucket about a foot in front of and a few inches to the right of your forward foot. Most of the balls should fall in that bucket.

Before you begin work on your toss, find out how high the ball must go for your serve. The ideal height is about 2 or 3 inches above the maximum height you can reach with your racket and arm fully extended. You should be ready to hit the ball just after it has started to fall, since it will be moving very slowly at that point and so will present an easier target.

The toss of the ball is not straight up. You should try for a gentle parabola out in front of you. The more aggressive your serve, the farther out in front you should toss the ball so that you'll be leaning into the serve as you make contact with the ball.

Since many players "throw" the ball into the air with a jerk that produces an erratic flight of the ball, it helps to think of "placing" the ball in the air instead of "tossing" it. You do not throw the ball up, you place it in position with a smooth and gentle release.

I don't think it makes much difference whether you hold one or two balls when you serve. I've always held two balls before starting to serve and never really questioned the habit. If you feel uncomfortable holding two, then put the second one in your pocket until you need it. Incidentally, in tournament play, you'll sometimes see a player throw away the other ball after a successful first serve. That can be distracting to an opponent and the umpire can require you to hang onto that second ball if your opponent complains.

Another habit among the pros is bouncing the ball before the toss. Jimmy Connors, for one, bounces the ball several times, often to the annoyance of his opponents, but that does help him set the rhythm of his serve. If bouncing the ball a couple of times helps you to concentrate on the serve, then fine, but don't make a fetish out of it. When I was younger I used to just walk up to the line and serve without giving it a second thought. Now, though, I find that bouncing the ball helps me relax a little and makes me focus my concentration on the serve.

HOW TO HIT A SLICE SERVE

Before I describe the service itself, I think you ought to develop a feel for the action of the service motion. If you have an old tennis racket, take it out on the tennis court, stand on the service line, and try to throw it over the far fence. At first you won't even be able to throw the racket as far as the fence. In fact, unless you've been playing a long time, I'll bet that you won't even be able to throw it over the net. However, you'll soon realize how much you must extend your body and how high you must throw the racket to get the distance. It's the same with the serve. You must extend your body and hit the ball out into the court—not down, because if you do that the ball will go into the net.

When you serve, your position on court is very important. In singles play you should normally stand as close to the center mark as possible, about 3 or 4 inches behind the baseline, but don't touch the line or you'll be foot faulting. By standing close to the center mark you're preparing yourself either to run straight up to the net or to stay back behind the baseline to defend. In doubles play you should move over to serve from the center of your half of the court. Again, that position lets you take the fastest route to the net. Of course, you can vary your serving position to get more angle on your serve, but that usually telegraphs your intentions to your opponent, who can also move over to cover the expected angled serve.

Stand with your forward foot at about a 45-degree angle to the baseline, your feet about shoulder-width apart and your rear foot parallel to the baseline. Hold your racket and the ball out in front of you and begin the motion of both arms together, allowing your arms to drop down and come up together in a very natural motion (see ball toss sequence photos on pages 37–39).

THE SLICE SERVE Side View

1 2 3 4

At first, don't worry about taking a long backswing on your serve. Just get the racket down behind your head in a smooth motion (frames 1 and 2) and concentrate on accelerating the racket head sharply upward and forward as you hit the ball. As you become more proficient at serving, your timing will improve and you'll be able to use a deeper "backscratching" motion for your serve (3). Chances are you'll be able to de-

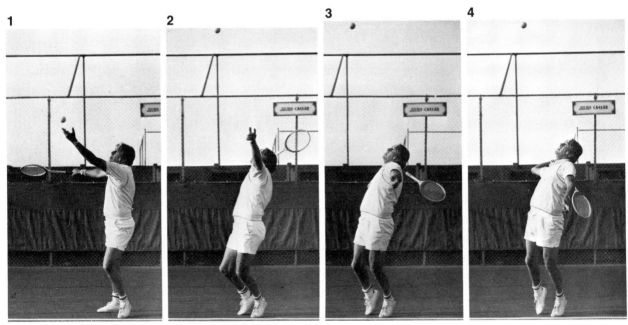

THE SLICE SERVE Front View

5   6   7   8

velop almost as much power with an abbreviated motion as with an exaggerated backscratching motion, anyhow.

Now your racket will be behind your head with your wrist cocked (4). Snap the racket up (5) and forward (6) so that the racket face moves from left to right behind and around the ball (7). If you're aiming into the deuce court, the direction of your racket at first will be toward the ad court. That may seem

43

THE SLICE SERVE Side View (continued)

9   10   11   12

wrong at the start, but you'll soon find that your racket is moving in an arc that pulls the ball around into the proper target area. The action is like the peeling of an orange as the racket goes around the ball.

You should hit the ball ahead of your body, leaning into the serve with your arm and body fully outstretched (8). Your weight will be completely on your forward foot and your rear

9   10   11   12

THE SLICE SERVE Front View (continued)

foot will come swinging through as you hit the ball (9), forcing you to take at least one step into the court. Follow through out in front of you (10), and let the racket swing through naturally (11) until it finishes up on the side opposite your hitting arm (12).

If you're hitting the ball well out in front, the natural motion of your body will make you take a second step into the court to maintain your balance. If you decide that the serve isn't good enough for you to rush the net, step back quickly so that you're about 2 or 3 feet behind the baseline ready to hit a ground stroke reply to your opponent's return.

The service action is like using a hatchet so that the blade accelerates to its fastest speed as it hits the limb of the tree. In the same way, the service motion calls for a snap of the wrist as you hit the ball. Try wielding a hatchet and then compare that action with your own service motion using a tennis racket.

HOW TO HIT A FLAT SERVE

Hitting a flat serve is no more difficult than hitting a slice serve. Hitting it where you want it to go, on the other hand, is more difficult because you don't have the spin that guarantees you a margin of safety over the net and ensures that the ball will curve into the court. By its nature the flat serve will go close to the net and you'll be relying on gravity to ensure that your serve does not go long. On the plus side, a flat serve will be fast and can often be an ace or a service winner. So it's useful to have a flat serve when you want to pull out all the stops on a first serve. But remember, you must have a good second serve to back up your first.

The motion of the flat serve is initially the same as for the slice in terms of the toss and the backswing. As you prepare to hit, you should turn your wrist back so that you hit the ball from behind with a flat racket face—just as though you were slapping a wall in front of you with the flat of your hand. Instead of the racket snapping across the back and side of the ball, the motion should be straight out in front of you toward the spot on the court you are aiming for.

When you hit a flat serve, one of your objectives should be to get plenty of power into it. I think you'll find it helps to think of the serve as a chain reaction starting from the backswing and going through the wrist snap into the hit. The last part of the chain reaction should be a snapping of the index and middle fingers in an effort to extract that last ounce of power from your motion. That final burst of power will give your flat serve the extra edge you'll need to hit the occasional ace.

HOW TO HIT A TOPSPIN SERVE

The topspin or American twist serve is considerably different from the flat and slice serves. It's a much harder serve to execute but because of its high, kicking bounce receivers often have trouble returning it. *Because the execution of the topspin serve demands more action from your back, I would not recommend it for any older player with a history of back ailments.* It's all too easy to damage weak back muscles with an incorrect or overly vigorous swing.

To hit the topspin serve you must toss the ball farther behind your head than for the flat and slice serves. You then arch your back and swing your racket back into a deep backscratching position. Swing the racket face from left to right up and over the ball with as much wrist snap as you can muster. Some players find that they can hit a topspin serve more easily if they follow through on the same side of the body as the racket hand. I personally don't recommend this because it's not a natural motion.

It's not likely that you'll be able to teach yourself the topspin serve, so I'd suggest you find a good teaching pro if you are really determined to learn this serve. If you can, I think you'll find the effort of mastering the topspin serve well worthwhile since it may often win the point if you mix it in with your normally sliced second serve.

THE SERVE AND RETURN OF SERVE

THE FOUR MOST COMMON SERVICE ERRORS

Most intermediate players make one very glaring mistake with the serve—they don't practice it enough. If you don't practice your serve, you can't expect to keep it at the peak of your ability. You must work on your serve constantly and that means getting a bucket of balls at least once a week—more often if you aspire to be a local tournament player—and practicing your serve for at least 20 minutes. Concentrate on practicing your second serve and your first serve will take care of itself. As I have said, a player is only as good as his second serve.

The second error I see among weekend players in particular is hitting the ball too hard. By going for extraordinary power you increase the chances of either netting your serve or hitting the ball out. Although I firmly believe you should try to win the point with the serve, it doesn't make any sense to keep losing points with your serve. If your serve is off for some reason, try taking a bit of speed off it by hitting with a little less force. I think you'll soon see your serves going in and doing so quite easily. At the same time, you might increase the spin on your serve to make doubly sure that the ball will go in.

Another faulty area for many players is the service toss. If you're hitting the ball erratically, chances are you're not tossing consistently to the same place each time. The only cure for this is to practice the toss until you can place the ball in the air with great consistency. If your toss suddenly becomes erratic during a match, you may be holding the ball too tightly. If so, relax your fingers as you toss so that the ball is released very gently into the air. That should give you a smoother toss.

Finally, *the fourth error I often see is that a player does not lean into the shot.* As you serve, all your weight should be on your front foot and you should be hitting the ball out in front so that you're leaning into the court as you make contact with the ball. If you're not leaning into the court, you should toss the ball farther out toward the net so you are forced to go forward to hit the ball. If you watch some of the top players in action, particularly John Newcombe and Arthur Ashe, you will see they lean well into the court as they deliver a powerful serve. If you are going to hit a serve with pace you must lean into the shot.

Serve Checklist

1. Take your time on the serve. You are in complete control of this stroke and the errors are entirely of your own making.
2. Hold the ball lightly in your fingers and place it in the air forward of the baseline.
3. Toss the ball a few inches higher than the highest point you can reach with your racket and arm outstretched.
4. Snap your wrist as you hit the ball.
5. Take one or two steps into the court for balance as you follow through.

THE RETURN OF SERVE

There is no simple formula for returning serve. The server has the choice of speed and placement and you, as the receiver, have to diagnose the server's intentions and decide on your own action in a split second. But, don't look upon the return of serve as a defensive shot. It isn't just a chance to stay in the point, but a chance to win the point, like any other shot in tennis. So, your choice of service return should be based on a decision to try to win the point with that shot if you can.

I prefer to return serve low over the net with as sharp an angle as possible. That way, I force the server to run hard to get to the ball, and, since the ball will be low when the server hits it, the shot will have to be hit up—a defensive shot—which will give me a chance to come in and hit a put-away volley. Now that kind of tactic is pretty hard since it calls for good strokemaking and rapid footwork. *An older person might prefer to stay back and hope the server's shot will be weak enough to give a good opportunity for a passing shot. In either case, you're setting up a situation where you have a good chance of winning the point.*

Of course, if the serve is hard and deep you may not be able to do much more than get your racket on the ball and keep the ball in play. If you are facing a hard server, I'd suggest you move back a little to receive serve and then merely block the ball back by taking a very short backswing for your return. You won't have time to go for a full ground stroke, so punch the ball as in a volley. You won't need the flowing motion of a normal ground stroke to put pace on the ball because you'll be able to use the pace the server has put on the ball.

Be careful about retreating for a return of serve. If the server has a good spin serve, the ball will curve farther away from you the farther you are behind the baseline. It will pay to take

a spin serve as early as possible so the curve is less pro-
nounced. When you hit a spinning ball, let the spin work for
you. Aim your return back directly at the server without at-
tempting to take the spin off the ball. The remaining spin will
cause the ball to curve away from the oncoming server, giving
you a good chance of a passing shot or a placement.

When the server faults on the first serve you have a very
good chance to win the point. For a start, the extra pressure
on the server to get the second serve in may result in a double
fault. Even if the serve is in, it will probably be weak and short.
In that case you should run in to make your return and run
around the ball to hit your strongest shot—the forehand for
most intermediate players. Here is a situation where you
should go for a low, angled placement to win the point.

To have a good return of serve you must get used to reading your opponent's serve as soon as the ball leaves the
racket. With practice against a variety of opponents you'll
soon become adept at diagnosing a serve and moving quickly
into position. When you're facing a left-handed server,
though, you may have a few problems because everything will
be reversed. For example, a lefty's slice serve will break to the
left instead of to the right. So when a lefty serves to your
backhand, especially in the ad court, you'll be pulled wide. In
that situation, move to the ball as quickly as possible and try
to stretch a little farther to get your racket on the ball.

For some reason, lefties seem to have a more natural slice
serve than right-handed players. When you are facing a lefty,
be prepared for a wider variety of spin shots on all strokes,
including the serve. I prefer to attack a lefty's serve by taking
it as early as possible before the spin has had much effect. If
you have doubts about your ability to do that, find a player
and practice together, especially on your backhand return of
serve, until you get a feel for the left-handed serve.

THE FOUR MOST COMMON
RETURN-OF-SERVE ERRORS

By far the worst error that most club players commit on the return of serve is to wait too long before moving to the ball. This is a question of both anticipation and rapid footwork. You must watch the server intently so that you can anticipate the direction of the serve and its spin. As the server hits the ball, it's a good idea to rise up on the balls of your feet to make sure that your weight is shifted and you're ready to take one or two quick steps forward. In fact, you'll often see a professional take a little hop as the server hits the ball. That hop helps the receiver start moving. As soon as the ball is hit—move!

Don't take too long a swing with your return of serve. You don't have the time to take a long backswing as though you were hitting a conventional ground stroke. And, because the serve will usually be coming at you very fast, you don't need the long swing to generate power for your return. Often a simple blocking shot will get the ball back over the net with enough speed to ensure that it will be effective. Abbreviate your backswing and concentrate on getting your racket on the ball out in front where you can control its direction.

Although it is not as common an error as the first two, *I often see intermediate players standing too far back when they receive serve.* The proper position is with your feet on the baseline, close to the singles sideline (see Chapters 7 and 8). If you're facing a cannonball server, then you can move back a couple of feet as the server hits the first serve. But if you move back for a spin serve, then you're letting the spin do its work and the ball will curve even farther away from you and be more difficult to reach. Always return a serve as early as you can.

A more general error is trying to do too much with the return of serve. Although I feel you should always look for a winning opportunity or a set-up situation with the return of serve, don't try to be too clever with this shot. Go for the cross-court ground stroke rather than a drop shot; go for a deep lob if you have to rather than an offensive lob that might be slammed back down your throat; and so on. If you are facing a good server, content yourself with keeping the ball in play. If you commit an error on the return of serve you have lost the point, but if you get the ball over the net you give your opponent the chance either to make an error or give you an easy set-up. So your return of serve should always be a shot that has a high percentage chance of success.

Return-of-Serve-Checklist

1. Watch the ball come off the server's racket.
2. Make your move as soon as you have read the serve.
3. Take a shorter backswing when you are facing a good server.
4. Hit spin serves as early as possible.
5. Move back to return a hard first serve.
6. Move up to return a weak second serve.

THE VOLLEY

THE VOLLEY

No matter what the level of your play, you must develop an aggressive net game. This means you must have reliable forehand and backhand volleys—shots hit before the ball bounces. *Even if you're an older player and don't rush the net after every serve, you will still find winning chances come most often when you can approach the net and end the point with a winning volley.*

Net play calls for a very alert ready position. You should be poised on the balls of your feet, ready to spring forward to attack a ball arriving above your waist, to crouch for a low shot, or to jump backwards if your opponent throws up a lob (see photo). Keep your racket up and out in front of you and keep your eyes on the ball.

I use a Continental grip for both forehand and backhand volleys. In the fast pace of top-level tennis there isn't much time to worry about changing grips when you're rushing the net, or in a rapid exchange of volleys. Even though the pace of your game may be slower I'd suggest you also use a single grip for both volleys. It's one less action to worry about when you're at the net.

Although you have less time to get in a set position for a volley than for a ground stroke, footwork is very important at the net. You should imagine you are flexed like a cat ready to take a couple of short, swift steps to get to a position where you can leap forward to attack the ball.

Chances are that you won't have time to turn your body completely sideways to the net with a final step toward the flight of the ball. If you do have time, make that final turn and step. If you don't, content yourself with pivoting your upper body so that your forward shoulder points to the ball. The hit itself is a short, punching stroke (see page 60) so you don't need a long backswing. The pivoting of your body will provide most of the backswing you need.

Always try to hit a volley out in front. I recommend hitting the ball at least 6 inches in front of your body. By hitting the ball early, you'll be able to keep your eyes on it all the time and you'll already be looking in the direction of your opponent in preparation for the return. If you let the ball get alongside or behind you, you won't be able to follow its flight, and may muff or miss the shot entirely.

You must keep a very firm wrist and forearm when you hit a volley. If you hit the ball with a loose wrist, you'll lose control completely. When I used to practice for a big tournament I would deliberately hold my wrist tighter than necessary, so that when I came to a critical volley in a match I would instinctively hold the racket firmly even if I were relaxing a little. Another must for hitting a powerful volley is to keep the racket head up, and keeping a firm wrist will guarantee that.

Many intermediate players can hit an effective volley when the ball is above the top of the net. It's much tougher to volley, though, when the ball is lower than the net, since you're forced to make a defensive shot by hitting up. If the ball is low, don't drop your racket head below your wrist or you'll lose firmness and make sloppy volleys that will give your opponent an easy putaway shot. Bend your knees and get down to the level of the ball's flight. That way, your eyes will be closer to the ball, increasing your chances of hitting it correctly in the center of the racket.

If you're faced with hitting a low volley, return the ball low over the net but hit it as deep as you can, so that your opponent will probably have to hit up. If you are alert you'll be able to get closer to the net for your next shot and put the ball away with no problem.

HOW TO HIT A FOREHAND VOLLEY

In a singles game, the best position for volleying is astride the center line about halfway between the service line and the net. If you're too far back you'll have to hit up on many volleys, giving your opponent some easy return shots. If you are too close to the net then your opponent will be tempted to lob over your head. In doubles you should volley from a position almost in the middle of the service box on your half of the court.

Wait for the ball with your knees bent and your body flexed like a coiled spring (frame 1). Keep your racket head up and in front of you. Don't take your eyes off the ball for a second. If you find you're having problems seeing the ball in the fast-paced action at the net, then crouch even lower so that your eyes move closer to the line of flight of the ball.

You'll be able to reach most volleys with a single step or by extending your reach a little. If you have to move farther to reach the ball, take short, sideways skipping steps but don't overrun the ball.

THE FOREHAND VOLLEY Side View

2   3   4

When you're sure of the direction of your opponent's shot, pivot the top half of your body, taking your racket back swiftly (2). The pivot of your body will give you almost all the backswing you'll need or have time for (3).

Hit the ball by punching forward (4) with a slightly downward stroke along the flight of the ball. Contact the ball about 6 inches in front of your eyes with your racket head above the level of your wrist (5).

Since you can use the speed that is already on the ball before you hit it, the volley doesn't require the long backswing and follow-through of a powerful ground stroke. Follow through out in front (6) in the direction in which you want the ball to go, but don't over-exaggerate the action. Follow through just enough to be sure that you can control direction (7, 8), and then recover for the next shot.

2   3   4

THE FOREHAND VOLLEY Front View

THE FOREHAND VOLLEY Side View (continued)

5 6 7 8

If the volley is high, you can hit it by punching down to angle it into your opponent's court. Your racket face should be almost vertical when you hit the ball. Make it a flat hit and don't try to put spin on the ball.

If you are faced with hitting a low volley, you'll have to open the racket face a little to hit up enough to get the ball over the net. In that case, I'd advise you to use a little underspin so that when the ball crosses the net and loses a little of its speed, it will float down and give your opponent a volleying situation that is tricky to handle. The underspin will help your control too.

5 6 7 8

THE FOREHAND VOLLEY Front View (continued)

HOW TO HIT A FOREHAND VOLLEY

The direction of your volley will be determined mostly by your body position. But you can also get direction by hitting the ball earlier or later. If you want to hit a volley down the line, lay your wrist back more than usual as you make the shot. This will help you hit the ball a little later, producing that down-the-line direction. If you want to hit crosscourt, don't lay your wrist back at all and you'll be able to take the ball earlier to get the crosscourt direction. Of course, you should also point the racket face in the direction in which you want the ball to go.

THE BACKHAND VOLLEY Side View

1   2   3   4

HOW TO HIT A BACKHAND VOLLEY

Many weekend players are as lax about their backhand volleys as they are about their backhand drives. The only solution is to practice and then practice some more. *In fact if, like many older players, you play mostly doubles, I'd suggest you spend more time practicing volleys than ground strokes.* Although I can volley equally well on either side, I think the backhand volley is easier because your racket arm is naturally in front of you as you hit, forcing you to hit the ball out in front—an essential principle of the volley.

You should be in a crouching ready position as you prepare to hit a backhand volley (frame 1). Be prepared to take one or two quick sideways steps to get to the ball. When you're in

1   2   3   4

THE BACKHAND VOLLEY Front View

6   7   8

position to take the shot, pivot the upper half of your body (2) to get your racket back to a position just behind your rear shoulder (3). Use your other hand to guide your racket back firmly (4) and to restrict yourself from taking too long a backswing. Remember, you don't have much time to hit a volley so you can't afford the luxury of a long backswing and a sweeping forward swing.

Punch the ball forward as though you were pulling a slingshot in your racket hand (5) and meet the ball about 6 inches in front of your forward hip (6). Keep your crouching position so that your eyes are close to the level of the ball's flight. Hit the ball flat, or with very little underspin, and follow through in the direction in which you want the ball to go (7, 8). If the ball is above the level of the net, you should be able to hit it down toward your opponent's feet. If the ball is lower than the net

6   7   8

you'll have to hit up, so concentrate on keeping the ball low over the net to prevent your opponent from hitting back down to you.

If a ball is aimed directly at your body, the best response is to hit a backhand volley. Just pull the racket in front of you and hit with a very short stroke. The pace of the ball will probably be enough for you at least to get the ball back over the net. You must keep your wrist firm when you're hitting that type of reflex volley. If you hit the ball with a weak wrist you'll have absolutely no control.

Many players are worried about injury from balls hit directly at them, especially during the close-quarters rapid action at the net. If you can, handle shots at your body with the reflex volley I've just described. If the ball is coming at your face you only have to move your head a few inches to one side or to duck. Better to miss the ball than to risk an eye injury. If you're afraid of being hit by a powerful overhead smash, then turn sideways and adopt what I call the "matador" stance. You'll present a smaller target for the ball and, chances are, it will hit only the fleshy part of your arm or leg, where it will certainly sting but cause little, if any, damage.

THE FOUR MOST COMMON VOLLEYING ERRORS

The biggest problem any player, young or old, amateur or professional, has with the volley is not watching the ball. At the net, the ball is moving very fast and is very close to you much of the time. You can't afford to let your guard down for a split second. Keep your eyes fixed on that ball so you can almost read the brand name as it comes toward you. You'll find you can see the ball more easily if you crouch down to get your eyes close to the level of the ball's flight. You'll be less likely to lose sight of the ball if you always hit your volleys out in front of your forward hip.

Taking too long a stroke for the volley is almost as common an error among weekend players. You don't have time to take a long backswing, nor do you need the power you get from the backswing you normally use for your ground strokes. Many players use too long a stroke for the volley because they have had far more practice in hitting ground strokes that call for a long backswing and a sweeping follow-through. Take a short backswing, meet the ball out in front, use an abbreviated follow-through, and your volleys will stay within the court with more than enough power.

The third common error is insufficient practice. How often do you go out to practice and spend 20 minutes on ground strokes, 2 minutes on the serve, 2 minutes on the overhead, and 2 or 3 minutes on your volleys? The proportions should almost be reversed. A few minutes hitting ground strokes will be enough to get you warmed up. You should spend 10 minutes hitting volleys, and 10 minutes each on the serve and the overhead. I can't overemphasize the importance of practice as the only way to develop confidence in your stroking. A half hour of practice each day will do your strokes more good than several hours of playing sets with your friends.

The fourth most glaring error, particularly of the nonprofessional player, is poor anticipation. Since there is little time to make decisions when you're playing at the net, you have to use every clue to guess your opponent's intentions so that you can get a fast start on making your next shot. For example, if you volley to the left you can expect the shot will be returned to your left. If I hit a volley to the left, I shift my weight so that I'm ready to move to the left as soon as my op-

ponent hits the ball. Players should also watch their opponents' rackets. If the racket slows down before your opponent hits the ball, or if the racket is coming up underneath the ball, be prepared for a lob and get ready to run back to hit an overhead. Observe these early warning signs and you'll be that all-important fraction of a second ahead in making decisions at the net.

Volley Checklist

1. Anticipate the direction of the ball by watching your opponent's stroke and racket movement.
2. Watch the ball by crouching down and getting your eyes close to the level of the ball's flight.
3. Use a short punching stroke with a brief backswing and an abbreviated follow-through.
4. Hit the ball in front of your forward hip for control and good eye contact with the ball.

THE OVERHEAD SMASH AND THE LOB

The lob and the overhead smash are the two most neglected strokes in tennis. They occur in sequence naturally in play. One player tosses up a high lob and his opponent responds by hitting an overhead smash. Many who have been playing tennis for years rarely make use of the lob and have never developed an adequate smash. But if you want to become a competent intermediate or advanced player, you can't afford to neglect either stroke.

For the older player, a good lob is vital. A high and deep lob will give you time to recover when you have been drawn out of position. By lobbing you'll be keeping yourself in the point, and that is most important in tennis.

The older player needs a competent smash to counter lobs. Although the smash is often thought of as a knockout punch, it does not require a devastatingly powerful stroke. In fact, *a smash generally requires much less power than a good flat serve because the ball gains momentum as it drops from the peak of the lob. So you can still develop a good smash although your muscles may not have the power of a younger player. Careful placement of a smash is worth more than power.*

Both the lob and the smash require that you watch the ball very carefully—that means regular practice of both shots.

THE OVERHEAD SMASH

Very few intermediate players have a good overhead smash. It's a difficult stroke because there is little margin for error. Few players get the chance to groove their overheads because there is so little chance to use the smash in a match.

THE OVERHEAD SMASH

But you can, and should, develop a good overhead if you practice the shot enough. In the days when I was practicing for a major tournament I might go out and hit one hundred or more overheads just to "get my eye in" for the shot. Although you may not have the time for that amount of practice, make sure you add the smash to your next practice session and always ask your opponent to throw up a few lobs in the warm-up session before your match.

Older players often hit poor overheads because they are not in position to make the shot. Although the arc of the overhead stroke resembles that of the serve, you have no control over the placement of the oncoming ball so you must continuously adjust your position with short steps to keep under the ball. You should watch the ball very closely as you hit so that you catch it in the center of your racket. An overhead does not require slice or spin—just a flat hit—so you can concentrate on hitting with the center of your racket. However, I use a slice swing quite often and you might like to try it also.

If you are an aggressive net player, your opponent will soon resort to a lob to force you back from the net. In this situation, I like to hit the overhead on the fly, provided that it is not a very high lob. If you hit the ball on the fly, you won't have to retreat so far and can quickly regain the net if necessary. If the lob is very high, you might as well let it bounce—it may bounce out. If your opponent's high lob is good, it will be moving more slowly after the bounce, and so will be easier to hit. If the shot bounces in you'll have plenty of time to get set for a more defensive shot than the smash. You can still hit a smash from the baseline, although it's unlikely to be a winner. You can also return the lob as a ground stroke.

1   2   3   4

HOW TO HIT AN OVERHEAD SMASH

The overhead motion is like the serving motion except for its much shorter backswing. The motion is as if you were throwing your racket over the back fence.

As soon as you see your opponent throw up a lob you should run back from the net to get behind the ball's line of flight (frame 1). If the lob is very high and deep you can let it bounce before hitting it. Otherwise, it's better to take the overhead on the fly. Watch the falling ball closely, taking short steps to adjust your position (2). The ideal position for hitting an overhead is under the ball so that if it continued to drop it would hit you right between the eyes.

Some players find they can sight the ball better by using their non-racket arm to point to the ball. By all means do this if it helps you. You'll have to get that arm out of the way

5   6   7   8

before you hit, of course. But since the action of getting your arm out of the way can help you start a forward body motion, it is useful in hitting the overhead.

Turn sideways to the net before you begin the stroke. Take your racket back behind your head until it's in a comfortable position (3, 4). Keep your head up and your eyes fixed on the ball (5). When the ball is 3 or 4 feet above your head, swing the racket forward (6, 7) and make contact (8, 9), with your body outstretched and both feet on the ground about shoulder-width apart. You should jump for an overhead only if you are forced to do so to reach the ball. Any shot you make with your feet off the ground is weaker than one hit with both feet firmly on the ground.

Hit the ball in the center of your racket and then hook it down into the opposite court, as you would with a serve (9). If you find you are hitting too many overheads into the net, practice the shot by aiming for the back fence, then gradually

73

9   10   11   12

hook the shot until you get a feel for the amount of downward motion needed to hit the ball in the court.

Allow the racket to follow through naturally (10, 11). The follow-through will not be as exaggerated as that of a serve, but the racket should end up on your non-racket side (12) and your weight should be entirely on your front foot as you complete the stroke. Then get into the ready position for your next shot.

It isn't necessary to change your body position to change the direction of a smash; in fact, this would only telegraph your action to your opponent. To place an overhead, hit the ball in the direction you want and follow through in that direction. I prefer to hit most of my overheads to my opponent's forehand since most players are slower in moving to the right than to the left. You should normally aim for the open court, although hitting a smash directly at your opponent will frequently confuse the player and give you the point.

74

COMMON OVERHEAD ERRORS

The overhead, handled correctly, is often a winning shot. You can hit the overhead with about half the speed you might use on a serve and you will still get enough pace on the ball to win the point, assuming you have an accurate placement. Speed is much less important than placing the ball where your opponent cannot reach it.

THE FOUR MOST COMMON OVERHEAD ERRORS

By far the worst error is not getting under the ball. You must keep moving so that you are always under the point where the ball would hit you between the eyes if it continued to fall. This requires judgment that you can gain only by practicing.

Although many players regard the overhead as a killing shot that ends a rally, *some are guilty of hitting their overheads so hard that the shot goes out of court or into the net.* Use less speed than you would use on a serve, concentrate on hitting the ball in the middle of your racket, and place your overhead in the open court. That way you'll be more certain of a winner than if you try to blast the ball out of the court.

A third common error is taking too long a swing. A long backswing makes for an overhead that is tough to time, with the result that the ball is mis-hit or missed altogether. A short, comfortable backswing is all you need. After all, you now know you don't need tremendous power for the overhead, so why take a long swing?

Many players take their eyes off the ball just before impact. There is a natural tendency to drop your head as you swing through the shot. Keep your head up so you can see the ball hit the strings. That way you'll be more certain of hitting the

THE OVERHEAD SMASH AND THE LOB

ball with the center of your racket. It doesn't matter if you lose sight of the ball just after it leaves the racket. You'll pick it up again before your opponent has a chance to make a return.

Overhead Checklist

1. Get under the ball so that it would hit you between the eyes if it continued to fall.
2. Let the ball bounce only if the lob is high and deep to the baseline.
3. Use a short backswing with a punching action to get the power you need.
4. Hit the ball into the open court or to your opponent's forehand side, where a player will have more difficulty in moving to make a return.

THE LOB

The lob is perhaps the most underrated shot in the intermediate player's repertoire. Few weekend tennis players can hit a deep and accurate lob because they rarely practice the shot. Yet, *a good lob is an invaluable weapon, especially for the older player, because many players have a poor smash and can't return the lob effectively.* Although you might think of the lob as a defensive shot, it can also be effective in forcing your opponents to make errors. Most of the time you'll want to use a lob when you are not in a good position to make an offensive shot. For example, lob when you are drawn wide out of court and want to give yourself time to get back into the center court position. Or, you might lob more offensively in doubles when your opponents are crowding the net and you want to force them to retreat. In either situation, you're not trying for a winning shot but one which has a good chance of keeping you in the point.

All you have to do with a lob is get it over your opponent's reach and deep enough so that it drops within a yard of the baseline. That will take practice. I suggest you practice by deliberately aiming for the baseline rather than just aiming to get over your opponent's racket. Go for depth and the height will more or less take care of itself.

The lob can be an offensive weapon. If you're in position to hit a good passing shot but are facing an expert volleyer, then hit a lob that just clears your opponent's racket and drops sharply in the back court. Timing is critical with this shot. You should disguise your stroke until the last second, then lift the ball quickly over your opponent's head. If well disguised, the offensive lob will catch your opposition by surprise and you'll have a very good chance of winning the point.

Some professional players, such as Rod Laver and Ilie Nastase, have a very good offensive lob with topspin. This shot drops rapidly in the court and kicks away sharply because of the topspin. However, the shot requires a strong wrist and a very quick wrist action that can be gained only from years of practice. *I don't recommend the topspin lob for older players whose wrists are not as strong or as flexible as they were.* The topspin lob is a low-percentage shot. Most of your attempts will go out and many of the ones that stay in will be so weak that they will be reached by your opponent, who may then hit a winner.

THE FOREHAND LOB Side View

1   2   3   4   5

HOW TO HIT A LOB

You should learn to hit a lob from both your forehand and backhand sides. Once you have a feel for the amount of lift needed to hit the ball to the opposite baseline, you should have few problems with either the forehand or backhand lob.

The footwork and backswing for the defensive lob are the same as for the forehand and backhand drives. As soon as you see that your opponent has put you in a defensive situation, get into position close to the expected flight of the ball and turn sideways to the net (frames 1 and 2). Take your racket back quickly (3) and swing forward with weight transfer, just

1   2   3   4   5

THE BACKHAND LOB Side View

as for the ground strokes. Remember to step toward the ball as you hit to get your forward foot across (4) and to help you transfer your weight forward.

As you make your forward swing, drop your racket head very slightly (5, 6) and open the racket face so that you can loft the ball into the air (7, 8). Keep the racket in contact with the ball for as long as possible and follow through upward so that your racket finishes high in the air (9, 10, 11, 12).

Watch the ball throughout the stroke and avoid the temptation of looking to see if your opponent is moving back to anticipate your lob. When you have decided to hit a particular stroke you should always continue with it. Never change your mind mid-swing.

10   11   12

The lob stroke is a lifting motion with the ball on the face of the racket. Hit the ball with a solid, smooth action like a ground stroke. Do not slap at the ball or slice it to make it go up in the air. If you practice your lobs every time you go out to play, you'll soon develop a feel for this lifting action.

For a defensive lob, you can hit the ball as high as you want, as long as it comes down inside the baseline. The higher you hit the ball, the longer you'll have to recover your position and get back into the point. A high lob will be moving pretty fast as it approaches your opponent, who will most likely let it bounce and may be hesitant about the return. However, on windy days keep your lobs lower to prevent the ball from

10   11   12

THE BACKHAND LOB Side View (continued)

being blown out of court or back into a more favorable position for your opponent. When you are playing indoors you'll have to limit the height of your lobs, of course.

If you are in a position to hit an offensive lob, disguise your stroke so that it looks like an attempt at a standard passing shot. Open the racket face at impact just enough to get the lob to clear your opponent's reach. Your lob has to be only 20–25 feet high to do just that. If you've disguised the shot, your opponent will be caught off guard and will have to scramble back to make a weak overhead at best.

After you have hit an offensive lob, you should be ready to go to the net and take advantage of the weak return that will probably result. After hitting a defensive lob, you'll most likely want to get back to the center of the court just behind the baseline to take care of the smash that may be coming your way. If your opponent has a really weak smash, you may be able to move up to the back line of the service court to return the smash.

THE FOUR MOST COMMON LOBBING ERRORS

The worst error you can make with a lob is to hit it too short. Your opposition will be able to run back and, most likely, have time to hit it on the fly. An opponent with a respectable smash will probably win the point. Ideally, your lobs should fall within a yard of the baseline. If your lobs drop repeatedly short, increase the length of your follow-through so that you are hitting through the ball for a longer time.

A common error I see among club players is a lob that appears to be aimed at the net player because the concern is only with getting the ball over the net player, rather than with hitting the lob deep. The closer you hit a lob to a player at the net, the higher the chance that your lob will be returned. This is a fault that you can cure only with constant practice. Ignore the player at the net and go for the line.

Don't give your intentions away too early. This happens with the offensive lob especially, where the idea should be to catch your opponent unaware. Make the lob look like a ground stroke or a passing shot until the last second before you contact the ball. Look at the ball and not the player so that your opponent will think you are concentrating on a passing shot. If you lift your head to check the player's position, you'll telegraph your action and invite a retreat.

The fourth error is not keeping the ball on the racket long enough. The lob is not a slice shot in which the racket is flicked behind the ball. You must hit a lob with a flat racket and hit through the ball just as you would with a forehand or backhand drive. The longer you can keep the ball on your racket, the deeper and more accurate your lobs. Again, practice is the only cure for this fault.

Lob Checklist

1. Aim for the baseline by hitting through the ball.
2. Disguise the shot by making it look like a ground stroke until the last moment before you contact the ball.
3. Watch the ball until you can see it hit the strings of your racket.
4. Follow through as high as possible.

6

THE ADVANCED STROKES

THE
ADVANCED
STROKES

The strokes presented so far form the basic armory of the tennis player. With that armory you can play a very good game of tennis. But, as you've probably realized, advanced players use a wider variety of shots, often because the nature of their play forces them into situations where the basic strokes can't be used, or simply because they have exceptional strokemaking ability. When you are confident that you have mastered the basic tennis strokes, you might like to add to your repertoire some of these advanced strokes: the half volley, the drop shot, the drop volley, and the lob volley. You might also wish to add spin to your shots. Be warned, though, that the more difficult the stroke, the lower your chances are of hitting it successfully. The more advanced strokes should be used only in situations either where you have no alternative or where you are absolutely sure of success.

THE HALF VOLLEY

Despite its name, the half volley is actually a ground stroke in which the ball is hit immediately after it has bounced. If you favor the serve and volley game you'll be faced with the need to half-volley quite often. If your serve is returned low to your feet as you rush the net, you will have to pause, scoop the ball over the net, and hope that you get it back well enough to stay in the point. The shot to use in that situation is a half volley.

The half volley is really a shot to avoid. It's just a device to get you out of an awkward situation—being caught in the "no-man's-land" between the baseline and the service box. You can avoid the half volley either by getting in faster so that your

THE HALF VOLLEY Side View

2   3   4

reply to the return of serve will be a conventional volley, or by staying back so that you can use a standard ground stroke. Except on very slow courts, I'd favor getting in to the net faster so that you can maintain the offensive. If you stay back, you'll be in a more defensive situation and you'll probably play a longer rally before you find a winning opening.

The key to hitting a good half volley, off either the forehand (frame 1) or backhand side, is to get down as low to the ball as you can. Your objective is to pick the ball up on your racket as close to the ground as possible. You can do this only if you bend your knees (2) so your rear knee is almost touching the ground. Since you'll have little time to execute the shot, you should take a very short backswing (2) as though you were about to execute a conventional volley with your racket close to the ground (3).

Contact the ball as soon as you can after the bounce (4), and just hit it up enough to get it over the net (5), hopefully

87

5   6   7

very low and deep so that your opponent doesn't get a chance to hit down and win the point. Chances are, your opponent will be moving up to net after forcing you to half-volley. If you aim the ball toward your opponent's feet, you can force a half volley return. To get the depth you must follow through (6) out in front as far as you can, just as you would with a ground stroke. You won't be able to get much pace on the ball but this shot doesn't call for power. It is a defensive shot in which you should be satisfied to make a return that will keep you in the point.

After you complete the shot (7), keep moving to the net. Since the half volley has put you on the defensive you should immediately get to a position closer to the net where you can take up the offensive.

I find that there are more half-volleying situations in doubles play where the receiver often hits a shorter ball for the return of serve. One of the basic principles of doubles, of course, is to force your opponents to hit up to get the ball back over the net. So you can expect that you'll have to hit up at times, which is where you'll need a half volley if you play against good doubles teams.

In singles the half volley is rarely used because one of the objectives of singles play is to keep the other player away from the net. For that reason, the return of serve will generally be deep to try to prevent the server from moving to the net. Occasionally you may receive a ball that bounces almost on the baseline, forcing you to use a half-volley-like shot to make any kind of return at all. Of course, you shouldn't be in that position because you should have moved back behind the baseline as soon as you realized that the ball was going to bounce deep.

THE DROP SHOT Side View

1   2   3   4

THE DROP SHOT

The drop shot is a deceptive "touch" shot hit from around the mid-court area so that the ball falls over the net out of your opponent's reach. Hit properly, the drop shot looks like a ground stroke until just before contact. Then, the racket encourages the ball just enough to get it over the net where it dies, bouncing close to the net. A correctly hit drop shot will bounce several times before it gets to the opposing service line. You'll need a skillful touch to hit a drop shot and you should be prepared to practice it faithfully before you try to use it in a match.

The drop shot is an excellent way to tire an older player who sits on the baseline and trades effortless ground strokes. On slow courts I often see senior players who have interminable

90

6 7 8

rallies from baseline to baseline. In that kind of a situation I look for a short ball so that I can get closer to the net and hit a drop shot that will force my opponent to run to the net. A series of drop shots will soon tire an older player.

To hit the drop shot, turn sideways (frames 1 and 2) as though you were about to hit a ground stroke and use the same backswing and forward swing you would for that stroke (3). The idea is to disguise the shot until the last minute so the other player can't anticipate the drop and start running to the net. Just before contact, drop the racket head slightly, open the face a little, and come under the ball, taking all the pace off it and pushing it gently in the direction you'd like the drop shot to fall (4, 5). Your wrist action in slicing under the ball should produce a little natural underspin so that the ball will float over the net and drop quickly on the other side.

Follow through out after the ball with your racket flat (6, 7, 8). The follow-through is flat and level with the racket at least

as high as the net. Don't hit the ball hard—the action is more like catching the ball on the face of your racket and lifting it gently over the net. If you hit the ball hard it will bounce deep enough for your opponent to run it down.

The drop shot is useful as a surprise weapon to break the rhythm of your opponent's game. There's nothing a good groundstroker hates more than to have a hard drive returned as a weak drop shot. The drop shot will force the baseline player to go to the net where you will, most likely, be able to counter with a passing shot if your opponent's volleying ability is weak.

If you have the skill you can hit a drop shot from anywhere in the court, but I think you'll find the shot easier if you use it from the mid-court area. You'll be in a position where your opponent is on the baseline and you'll have the choice of hitting an approach shot (a shorter ground stroke) and continuing to the net or using a drop shot to force your opponent to the net. Use the drop shot only when you are pretty sure you can place it just over the net. If you hit the drop too deep, your opponent will not have to come in quite so far and will have an easy chance for a passing shot.

Practice the drop shot off both your forehand and backhand sides by getting your practice partner to hit short balls that land near the back line of the service court. Constant practice is required to maintain the delicate touch and the deception essential for its use. However, once you have the feel for the drop shot, avoid using it often. The drop is a surprise shot, to be used only a few times in a match. Use it too often and the element of surprise will be lost.

THE DROP SHOT

THE DROP VOLLEY

THE DROP VOLLEY Side View

1 2 3 4

THE DROP VOLLEY

The drop volley is a much tougher shot than the drop shot simply because of the tremendous touch required. It is a drop shot hit in a volleying situation so that the ball just barely crosses the net. It falls so quickly that it either can't be reached or it forces your opponent to hit up, giving you a chance for a putaway volley. Remember that if you are in position to hit a drop volley, you could also hit a regular volley—a much higher percentage shot. So you must be sure of your ability to hit this shot before you attempt it in match play. The shot can be a perfect winner if it's used properly. If not, it can be a perfect loser.

To hit the drop volley, prepare as though you were about to hit a conventional volley (frames 1–4), but as you stroke the ball bring your racket head underneath it (5) and take all the

6   7   8

pace off the ball (6). Use a little backspin (see the last section in this chapter) and push the ball very gently so that it angles sharply over the net, well away from your nearest opponent.

Contact the ball with a caressing action—you should be trying to take the pace off the ball so that it has just enough speed to take it over the net. There is practically no follow-through on this shot (7, 8)—all the work is done by the time the ball leaves your racket.

I enjoy using the drop volley but I probably devote ten times as much practice time to this shot as any other top player. Unless you have exceptional touch or are prepared to devote a lot of practice time to this shot, I think you'd be better off avoiding it. *Many older players develop good touch in compensation for decreasing muscular strength. If you do have good touch, by all means try the drop volley.* If you can do it, you'll have lots of fun when it's successful.

THE LOB VOLLEY Side View

1   2   3   4

THE LOB VOLLEY

On rare occasions in playing doubles when all four players are at the net, you may use a lob volley to force your opponents away from the net. It's a shot you should use rarely and then only when the other team is returning your normal volleys easily. Like the drop volley, the lob volley calls for great touch—not an easy stroke to execute in the fast action of doubles net play. The chances of making an error with the lob volley are pretty high; use the shot only when you have great confidence in your touch.

To hit a lob volley, you prepare as though you were about to hit a conventional forehand or backhand volley (frames 1–3). As you bring the racket forward, open your racket face (4) to hit under the ball (5) and then attempt to punch it over your opponent's head (6). Keep your wrist firm and use a stiff arm

5 6 7 8

to get a punching motion as though you were about to deliver a knockout uppercut to your opponent's jaw.

Don't be afraid to hit the ball firmly so that it clears your opponent's racket easily (7, 8). If you make the mistake of hitting the lob volley too gently you'll give the opposition a perfect chance to hit a high volley either at your feet or directly at your body. A poor lob volley will almost guarantee that you'll lose the point. A good lob volley will catch your opponents by surprise and let you keep the offensive at the net.

It's rare to see the professionals using the lob volley—they know what their opponents will do to a poor lob volley. However, if you have good touch, the lob volley might make an effective surprise weapon to use once or twice in a match. But if your opponent slams the shot back in your face, don't try it again.

97

THE USES OF SPIN

I am often asked why I rarely advocate using spin, especially when many older players with a variety of spin shots seem to do well against younger opponents. I can, of course, put spin on my serve, ground strokes, and other shots as can any top player who has spent day after day for many years hitting tennis balls. But I think it's important for the beginner to learn how to hit the ball flat at first. You can get all the power, control, and accuracy you'll need by hitting the ball flat (with the possible exception of the serve) and you'll make far fewer errors than if you try to use topspin or backspin on all your shots. When you have thoroughly grooved all your strokes and consider yourself a good intermediate player, then you might consider using spin when the occasion calls for it. However, you can still be an excellent player without spin shots. Jimmy Connors, for example, hits almost all his strokes with no spin.

The one shot where spin is a definite advantage is the serve, especially in doubles play. It's crucial to get your first serve in when playing doubles, and a spin serve (see Chapter 3) will leave you a greater margin for error than a flat cannonball serve. If, as I suggest, you use a backhand grip for the serve, chances are you'll have a natural slice action that will help the ball drop faster in the court and make it veer to one side after bouncing. For myself, I favor the topspin or twist serve as a second serve because the topspin brings the ball down more sharply, ensuring that the serve goes in, and causes the ball to kick after bouncing. The kick makes the receiver's job just that much harder.

For the ground strokes, there are two ways of developing topspin. One is a natural action in which the racket face stays nearly vertical through the shot but your arm action brings the racket up from below the flight of the ball. The movement is like brushing the rear face of the ball. Many players develop a slight topspin action of this type naturally, especially on the forehand side. If you already have this action, then stay with it and use it when you have to. A little topspin is useful when you're playing with the wind behind you and you want to be sure that the ball will drop easily in your opponent's court. You might also use it when you want to hit a shorter ball to your opponent.

The second way to get topspin on ground strokes is to use the natural action combined with a sharp wrist movement that rolls the racket over the top of the ball. This can put devastating topspin on the ball, but it's a very difficult action. You need a wrist as strong as Rod Laver's or Bjørn Borg's to copy their topspin shots. I wouldn't even suggest an older player try that topspin action.

The reverse of topspin is slice, or underspin, in which the racket starts a little higher than the ball's flight and ends up below the ball's flight. It's hard to get any power into a sliced shot and even harder to get effective control. The ball will come off the racket very slowly and float over the net. Hit well, an underspin ball will drop sharply once it gets over the net so the shot is a good one when you want to bring your opponent up to the net, or if you're returning serve to the feet of the on-coming server.

The big problem with a sliced ball is that it's moving slowly, which will give an older player more time to get to the ball either before or after it bounces. If you slice your return of serve in doubles, you're giving the net player a chance to come across and poach on the floating ball. A sliced ball must be kept low over the net, and that calls for more control than most older intermediate players possess. Go ahead and experiment with the slice, but use it only when you're sure you can make it.

SINGLES STRATEGY

SINGLES STRATEGY

There's no doubt that the singles game is the toughest version of tennis mainly because the player has to cover all the court. To play top-level singles you must have a powerful stroke, fast footwork, and a good volley backed up by some very solid ground strokes—in short, singles calls for an all-court style of play. To win at tournament singles play, you must be aggressive and take advantage of each opportunity presented. Almost always that means the best singles players are young, have powerful strokes, and tremendous agility on the court. But the older player can still make a good singles competitor by recognizing his or her limitations and playing a thinking game.

To play a thinking game there are a few rules you should keep in mind and check off mentally when things seem to be going against you in a singles match. A younger player can almost blast an opponent off the court with a strong serve and a net-rushing game. The older player can't do that, so file these rules in your head and refer to them when your game needs an extra edge.

SINGLES STRATEGY POINTERS

Always get the ball back. You won't lose the point if you hit the ball over the net so that it lands fairly in your opponent's court. Most points in tennis are won on errors rather than on outright winners, so give your opponent every chance to commit such errors. Don't hand the ball point to your opponent on a platter, though; get the ball back deep and to your opponent's weakness if you can.

SINGLES STRATEGY POINTERS

Go for the corners. In singles, especially against a baseline player, hit the ball deep and to the corners. Your objective is to make your opponent run for the ball. Not only will you tire the other player, but you'll increase the chances that your opponent will hit a weak shot allowing you to come up on the ball and go for a placement or hit a tough shot that will force an error or put you in a better position at net.

Aim for the weakness. If you know your opponent has a poor backhand drive or a weak overhead smash, hit to the weakness. Force the other player to use the backhand or hit overheads. By concentrating on that weak shot you'll increase the chances of your opponent's making an error and you'll be destroying his or her confidence at the same time.

Force your opponent to hit up. Any time your opponent has to hit a ball from below the level of the net, the shot will have to be hit up just to get the ball over the net, and such a defensive shot carries less power and speed than one hit down. When you're at the net you'll be able to hit down on most of the shots your opponent has to hit up, so you should hit low shots that force a hitting-up situation.

Return the ball early. Hit the ball as soon as you can, don't wait for it to come to you. If possible, the best time to hit the ball is as soon as it comes over the net. If you're back on the baseline, move up to hit so you can go to the net when you get half a chance. Look out for the short ball that lands around the service line. Move up on that ball and go to the net. Even if your footwork isn't what it used to be, a short ball, returned properly, will still give you time to get to the net.

Always change a losing game. If you're outclassed by an opponent, try changing your tactics. If you've been staying on the baseline, go to the net. If you haven't been lobbing, start using the lob. Use any strategy you can to put your opponent off. There's no point in changing a winning game, but there's everything to be gained from changing a losing game.

SINGLES STRATEGY

Try for deception. If you blast away at the ball, your opponent will probably anticipate that a deep shot is coming and prepare accordingly. If you hit your hard and soft shots in the same way, your opponent will have a much tougher time figuring out where the ball is going to go. Disguise all your shots as much as you can so that your opponent can't figure out their direction and pace until the ball is well off your racket. That way, your opponent will have less time to make an effective return.

My own preference for singles strategy has always been to get the first serve in hard and deep, and then to follow that serve to the net to put away the first or the second volley. Even when receiving in singles, my philosophy is to take the return as quickly as possible and get up to net. *However, as I get older, getting to the net is not as easy as it was, so now I wait sometimes and look for the opening—the short ball—that will let me go to the net with safety.* There's no point in rushing the net only to be passed before you can hit the first volley.

I think the older player should be able to play a baseline game and know the situations when it's possible to take control of the net. Also, a singles player should know how to defend against a net rusher and how to beat a consistent baseline player. To give you some ideas on singles strategies I'm going to run through some typical singles points: the serve and volley game, staying back after serving, facing a net rusher, and beating a baseliner.

There are, of course, many more strategies than the four simple ones I'm about to show you. Most of your points will not work out exactly the way I describe but I hope these examples will give you ideas for planning your own points—for developing the thinking game I feel is essential for the older player. Take the ideas I'm going to give you as a basis for your own planning and I'm sure you'll develop winning strategies of your own. You can develop further by watching top players on television, especially at those tournaments played on clay where the pace is relatively slow and the rallies longer so that you can appreciate the sequence of a point.

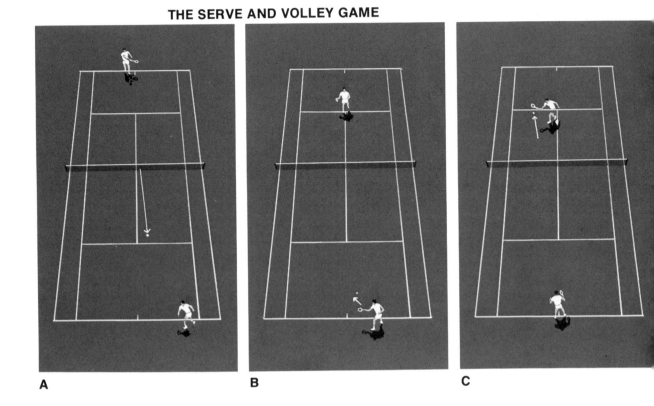

A   B   C

THE SERVE AND VOLLEY GAME

Rushing the net calls for a good, deep serve and a fast start on moving up to the net. You'll usually want to rush the net only behind your first serve and, for the older player, only when you're sure you can hit a good serve. Between the time you hit your serve and when the ball reaches your opponent's racket, you should be about 15 feet into the court. If you can't get as far into the court as you'd like, try hitting your serve with a little less pace and more spin. A three-quarter speed serve with lots of spin will give the older player more time to get to the net.

If you're serving into the deuce court (Fig. A), I recommend you normally hit your serve down the center. A down-the-center serve has two advantages. First, your opponent will have a smaller range of angle for the return, and second, if

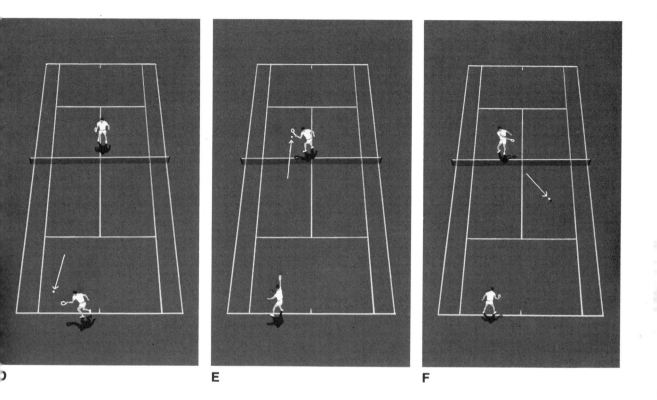

D   E   F

your opponent is a right-hander, you will be going for the backhand, which is generally a weaker stroke for most intermediate players. Follow your serve toward the net—generally along the line taken by the ball—and pause for a second as your opponent hits the ball (B).

That pause will help you concentrate on diagnosing the direction of the return, and you'll be ready to move either left or right to reply to the return of serve. If we assume that the receiver hits the ball crosscourt slightly (C), you should move to the right and be prepared to make your first volley, advancing as you start to make the shot. Chances are you'll have to hit up a little on the first volley, so concentrate on getting the ball back deep and down the line (D), and move toward the center of the court as soon as you've hit it.

If the receiver has stayed back, he will have to hit the ball up (E), which will give you a perfect chance to hit down on the ball. You should angle the volley for a placement (F).

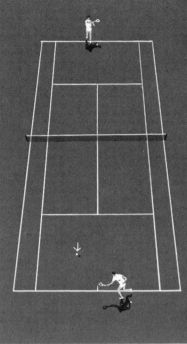

A   B   C

STAYING BACK AFTER SERVING

Any time you have to use a second serve, or your serve is less effective than usual, you should consider staying back after serving and waiting for the right chance to approach the net. You may even win the point from the baseline, especially if you're playing on a slow surface like clay. If you decide to stay back, remember patience is a great virtue in the back court.

There are basically two ways of winning from the back court. You can rally back and forth with deep ground strokes to either corner of the court, gradually pulling your opponent out of court to give you an open area into which you can hit a winning shot. That is a strategy you will often see among top women players on clay. It calls for precise ground strokes like those of Chris Evert. But a rally like that can go on interminably until the set-up is made. An older player might find long rallies that call for chasing the ball up and down the baseline

108

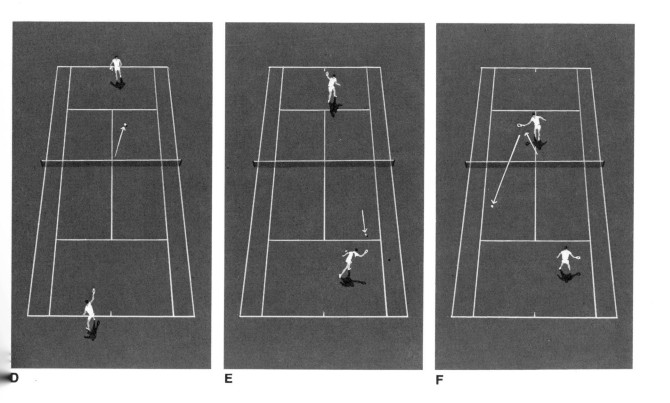

D   E   F

too tiring. For that reason, and because I think aggressiveness pays in singles, I prefer to look for the short shot that will get me started on the way to the net.

Suppose, for example, you are making your second serve to the deuce court. Hit the serve down the middle (Fig. A) and stay back a couple of feet behind the baseline, close to the center mark (B). If the return comes crosscourt—as it might— on your forehand side, you have a good chance to set up an approach shot that will help you get to the net. Hit the forehand deep to your opponent's corner (C) and return to the middle of the base line as soon as you can, ready to move in any direction. If your opponent has to run wide, a weak shot may result that lands close to the service line (D). Run up, take the ball early with a down-the-line ground stroke (E), and continue to the net. Your opponent will have to scramble for that return and be forced to hit up, and you'll then be in a good position to put the volley away (F).

109

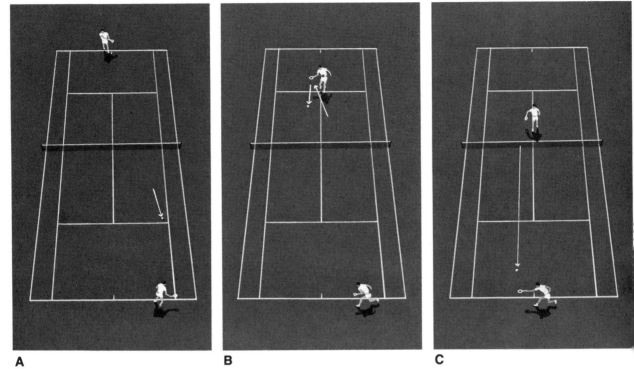

A   B   C

DEFENDING AGAINST A NET RUSHER

Now let's suppose that you're facing a server who always comes to net behind a powerful serve. What are your options? You are in a defensive situation, so you must concentrate on getting the ball back over the net to stay in the point. Your best percentage shot will be to get the ball back low. You'll then have to stay back and wait for an opportunity to hit a passing shot or a lob to win the point. A good lob will push your opponent away from the net so that you can use a passing shot. If you have the ability, you can counterattack by rushing the net yourself, but I think you should leave that to the younger and more foolhardy players.

Defending against a net rusher calls for a percentage game: hit the shots you know you can make. If you are receiving in the deuce court and your opponent serves to your forehand (Fig. A), return low and crosscourt—preferably to the oncoming

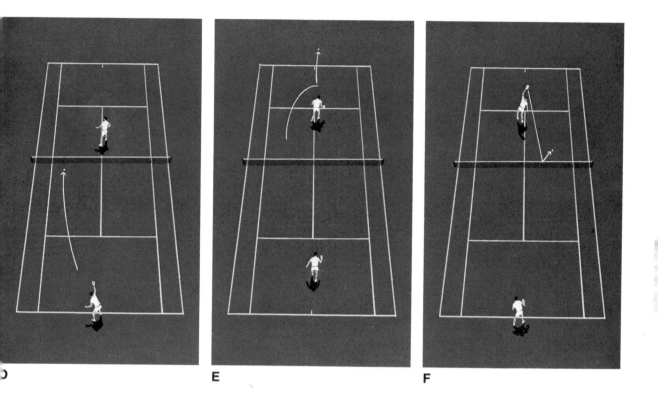

server's feet. Return to the middle of the baseline as quickly as you can. The server's first volley (B) is likely to be a fairly slow shot, especially if your return was low over the net. So you should have time to get set for either a passing shot or an offensive lob (C).

Since the server will be continuing to the net, disguise your shot until the very last second. If you have a good low ground stroke, hit a passing shot. If not, hit an offensive lob over your opponent's head and prepare yourself for the smash. A properly hit offensive lob will catch your opponent off guard, so use it often (C). If the smash is short, you may be able to move up on the ball and continue to the net (F).

The key to defending against the net rusher is to use control on all your shots. You don't need depth since the other player is close to the net. But you do need accurate placement of the return of serve, passing shot, or lob.

111

BEATING A BASELINER

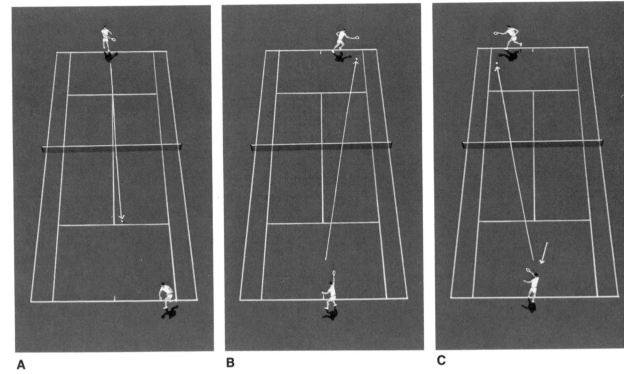

A   B   C

BEATING A BASELINER

If most of your opponents are older players who have had several years' experience in playing the game, you will inevitably come up against the crafty kind of player who sits on the baseline and lobs and dinks you to death. That kind of player will have you running all over the court. Such players rarely make an error, while their opponents tire themselves out by mentally and physically playing a style they don't like. How do you beat such a player?

Most baseliners play from the back court for a very simple reason—they don't like to play at the net. They may be afraid of net play because they have a weak volley or they may not have the speed to get up to net quickly. Either way, your strategy should be to force the baseliner to the net. Use the drop shot to bring the player up and hit a passing shot. If the base-

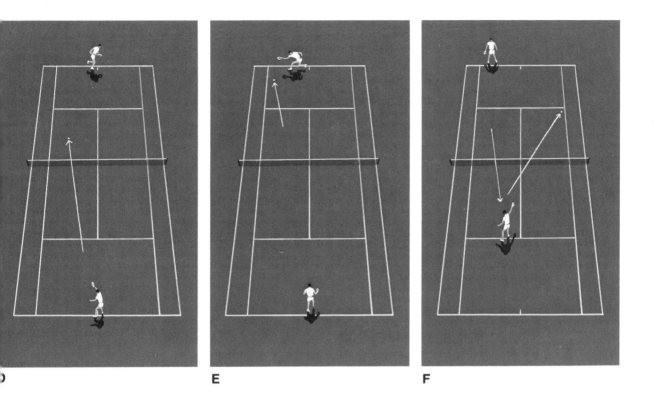

E F

liner's volley is strong but that player is slow around the court, use a drop shot to bring your opponent up and a lob to get him or her to move back.

Another technique to use against a baseliner is "wrong-footing." By this I mean setting up a pattern of ground strokes and then deliberately hitting behind the player to catch your opponent going the wrong way. You can often use this technique with a baseliner who likes to settle in for long rallies. Suppose you're facing a baseliner who serves down the middle into the deuce court (Fig. A). Return the serve down the line (B), and then go for the opposite corner (C). On your next return, turn your body as though you're about to hit to the opposite corner. If the other player begins to move, hit the ball behind your opponent so that he or she has to make the shot by turning around and, literally, hitting off the wrong foot (E). Chances are that player will mis-hit the shot or give you an easy shot to make a winner (F).

Baseline players often get stuck in a groove. Anything you can do to disturb that groove will help you win the point. Remember, too, that baseline players often have a weakness. Find that weakness and exploit it.

FOR THE OLDER SINGLES PLAYER

Many older players favor the doubles game because it's usually much less exhausting than singles. But there's no reason why you shouldn't continue to play singles, against opponents of similar ability, for your entire tennis career. The singles game you'll be playing won't be the same as that of a twenty year old but it can be challenging and enjoyable. Singles does not have to be an endurance test, so change your game accordingly. Here are a few suggestions:

Use your body weight. You'll put more power into your shot if you transfer your weight as you hit the ball. Let your body do the work instead of tiring your arm and shoulder muscles. Don't try to force your shots.

Don't be rushed. Take your time between serves, between points, and between games. Deliberate stalling can be annoying but no one will object to a steady pace that will give you breathing space between points, serves and games.

Watch the score. Don't waste your energy chasing the ball when you are down love–40. If you overextend yourself you may suffer by losing the next few points. Save yourself for the next game.

Get your first serve in. Serving twice calls for almost twice as much energy as serving once. Conserve your energy by getting your first serve in often.

Never neglect your strengths. You should have one or two shots that you can rely on to get the ball back easily and accurately. Polish these strokes so they are instinctive when you need them.

Keep fit. It takes twice as much effort to stay fit at age forty as it did at age twenty. Playing tennis alone will not keep you fit. You'll need a conditioning program to go with your tennis play. You should also have a regular physical and coordinate your exercise program with your doctor.

8

DOUBLES STRATEGY

DOUBLES STRATEGY

Although I still prefer to play a tough singles game and I got the most satisfaction from winning the world's top singles titles, I have always enjoyed doubles play and find myself enjoying the doubles game more as I grow older. Doubles doesn't call for the same fast footwork and stamina that's required for singles play, but it does require precise shotmaking and the use of your brains. So the older player can excel at doubles and maybe derive more satisfaction from this than from singles play. Doubles is no less exciting than singles. There's little in any other sport that can compare with the rapid action of four players firing volleys back and forth across the net.

Doubles is definitely the thinking person's game—it calls for teamwork, for the two partners to know and understand each other, and for good communication between the players. Consequently, it's important that a doubles team be aware of the basic strategies of doubles play and that each player know the other's game well enough to develop more advanced strategies. In this chapter I'll show you some of the simpler doubles strategies, after we've taken a look at the basic principles of doubles play.

First and foremost, you and your partner must play as a team. Agree before you begin play on who will go back for the overhead smashes, who will take the balls that come down the middle, and when you will encroach on each other's territory (for example, when poaching on service returns). Move around the court together so that you don't leave any large holes that will give your opponents an easy putaway shot. For example, if the player nearest the net moves over to the right to take a shot that is coming down the alley, the other player should also edge over to the right to help cover the part of the court opened up.

To help good teamwork along, partners should talk to each other. Encourage your partner as much as possible, especially

DOUBLES STRATEGY

if things are not going too well. I remember playing with Kenny Rosewall many years ago when he was having an off day. For four and a half sets I had to carry Rosewall—in fact, I would rather have played with my own seven-year-old son that day. However, I kept telling Kenny that his confidence would come back and sure enough, in the fifth set, it did and we went on to win the match. Even the best players can have an off day.

You should also tell each other your plans. If you're facing a player who consistently returns serve crosscourt, you'll probably want to try a poach where the net player moves over to volley the return of serve. Tell the server before you try it or you'll both be going for the same ball and you may end up losing rather than winning the point. You don't need a steady stream of chatter—a few words every now and again will be enough.

Doubles is a game that is won at the net. You'll win more doubles points if your team is in control of the net for the very simple reason that the closer to the net you are, the easier it is to volley downward and either put the ball away or force your opponents to make an error in hitting up. So the server should always follow his serve to the net. And the receiver should return serve low so that the return can be followed to the net if possible.

Once at the net, the key to winning the point is to keep the ball low and force your opponents to volley up. A ball that is rising as it comes over the net can be volleyed down for a putaway. Although it's certainly necessary to have a powerful volley for those putaway shots, you should also practice taking the pace off your opponents' volleys so that the ball will drop low and short. If you have the ability, the drop volley is a very useful shot in doubles, but not when your opponents are at the net.

Unlike singles, doubles is not a game where you are con-

stantly looking to win the point with the next shot. Your approach should be to keep the ball in play either to set up a winning situation or to force your opponents to make an error. Many doubles teams find an effective strategy is for the player with the better "touch" shots to hit the set-up and for the player with the more powerful volley to hit the winning volley.

Similarly, the serve is not the devastating weapon that it is for singles play. Your objective with a doubles serve is to get the first serve in with medium pace and good depth, preferably to the receiver's weakness. The majority of first serves should go deep to your opponent's backhand to make the return as difficult as possible. Great concentration is required for that first serve. I often hear players complain that they're having trouble getting their first serve in, yet they rarely seem to double fault. That's because they concentrate much harder on getting the second serve in—they don't want the embarrassment of losing the point on a double fault. Concentrate on your first serve as if it were a second serve and you'll get most of your first serves in. Of course, it almost goes without saying that you must have a reliable second serve, too.

If anything, the return of a serve is almost as important as the serve. Don't try to do too much with your return of serve. Concentrate on getting the ball back over the net at the feet of the oncoming server who is rushing the net. The closer you can get your return to the server's feet, the more difficulty the server will have getting the ball over the net. It also pays to keep the return of serve low over the net so that the opposing net player will have less chance to run over and poach on the return. Don't cut it too fine—it's better to stay in the point than to net your return of serve.

Finally, if you want to do well in doubles, learn to lob, lob well, and do it often. Whenever you're facing an aggressive doubles team that constantly takes the net, lob deep into the back court. You'll get the other team away from the net and you'll ensure a little breathing space to reposition yourselves for the next shot. *I think that is especially important for the older player. A lob will give you time to get into position so that you can stay in the point and, hopefully, get back into that controlling net position.* Nowadays, I find that a server who can angle a serve so that I'm pulled out of court is tougher to counter because I can't run back into position as fast as I used to. My answer to that kind of serve is to toss up a high lob into the opposite corner of the court. Not only do I have time to get back into the court, but I also stop the server from rushing the net. So never neglect your job and re-member that most older players have relatively weak over-heads.

DOUBLES STRATEGY

STARTING THE POINT

When I watch club players I often see a doubles team lose a point just because the players didn't take up the proper positions on the court to start with. So here are my suggestions for your starting positions.

When serving, you should stand approximately halfway between the center mark and the singles sideline. From that position you'll have the shortest distance to run to get to the net and cover your half of the court. If you're the server's partner, you should stand about 6 feet from the net and near the singles sideline. From this position cover all the volleys and, if necessary, back up to cover the lobs. Of the four players on the court, the server's partner is the one who is already in the perfect position for net play.

On the receiving team, the receiver should stand on the baseline close to the singles sideline. In the deuce court you might stand almost on the singles sideline, especially if you are facing a spin server. Don't go more than a few inches behind the baseline or you'll be giving a spin serve more time to curve even farther away from you. If possible, try to attack the serve by taking the ball early and you'll be in a better position to follow it to net. The receiver's partner should stand in the service box about 6 feet from the net and close to the singles sideline. If your partner hits a low return at the server's feet, you will both be able to move forward to take control of the net.

The positions I've described are the ones to take up only when the server prepares to hit the ball. Be ready to move as soon as the server hits the ball. He should start to move to the net for the first volley. And, as soon as the receiver makes a return, the other players should be ready to adjust their positions. George Lott, a famous doubles player of the twenties and thirties who used to partner all-time great Bill Tilden, claims that one of the secrets of doubles is to move as soon as the ball is hit. He's absolutely right. If the ball is hit to the left, your team should move to the left almost as though the two of you were connected by a 12-foot rope. If your partner goes back for a lob, drop back a little until you can both go to the net again. Whatever happens on the court, keep moving.

Now let's see where you should move by taking a look at some typical doubles strategies.

A   B   C

GETTING TO THE NET

If you win the toss and elect to serve, start the match with your most reliable server. In the first game especially, the server should concentrate on getting the first serve in, and both of you should concentrate on keeping the ball in play. Let your opponents make the mistakes, especially while they are not warmed up.

Assuming that all the players are right-handed, your first serve should go down the middle to the receiver's backhand (Fig. A). Serving into the ad court, you can also go for the backhand although this will give the receiver a greater choice of angle for the return. Still, a backhand crosscourt return can be tough, especially if the receiver has been pulled wide by a spin serve. Vary your serve by occasionally hitting to the receiver's forehand. That will stop the receiver from anticipating

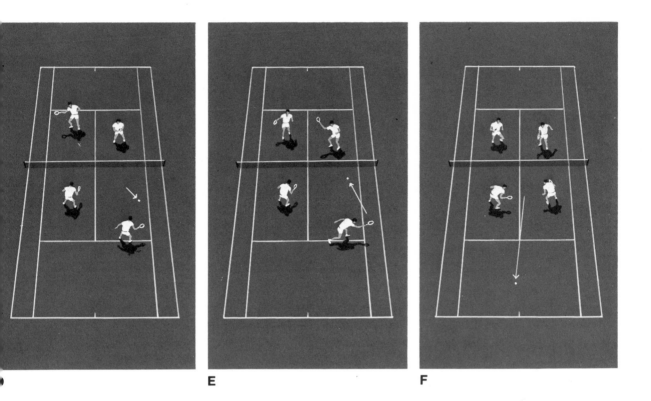

E   F

your serve and running around it to use a stronger forehand stroke.

Follow your serve toward the net (B) and hesitate momentarily as the receiver hits the ball. By hesitating, you'll be able to diagnose the direction of the return and make your next move accordingly. If the return goes down the line, you'll be able to continue toward the net. If, as in the sequence illustrated here, the return is crosscourt (C), you'll want to move up a little to hit the first volley.

For the first volley, your best bet is to hit the ball at the person who is farthest away from the net, so make your volley toward the feet of the oncoming receiver (D), who will probably be approaching the service line on his half of the court. If the ball is low to the receiver's feet, he'll be forced to hit the ball up (E), giving the other team a chance to hit a winning volley (F).

USING A LOB

A   B   C

USING THE LOB

Of course, many points will not work out in the simple way I've just described. So let's consider a situation where you're facing an aggressive team that takes control of the net and forces your team to take up a defensive baseline position.

In this case, I'll assume that the opposing server hits the serve wide to the receiver's forehand (Fig. A) and immediately rushes the net. The receiver's scrambling return is intercepted at the net by the net player, who volleys to the receiver (B). Now the receiver is faced with a problem. There has hardly been time to get back to a baseline position and the two opponents are well up at the net, ready to kill any weakly hit ground stroke.

The answer here is to lob high and deep (C). A high lob will give the receiving team time to recover for the anticipated

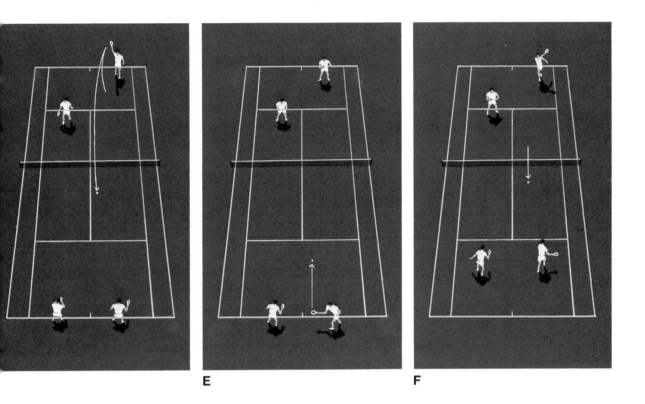

E   **F**

smash and the depth will force at least one of the opposing team to retreat to the baseline (D). At this point it is unwise for the receiving team to rush the net unless both members of the other team have weak overheads. The receiving team should stay back to take the smash (E) and wait for a short shot (F) that will give them the chance to move up to the net.

Using the lob has not only kept the receiving team in the point, but it has also reminded the other team that they can't afford to get too close to the net as they may not be able to move back in time to hit the lob. A high and deep defensive lob will, of course, usually give one player enough time to cover the shot; but a lower, more offensive lob could have been used in this situation and could well have been a winning stroke. When you're forced to hit a lob from a deep position, it's best to hit a defensive shot, but if you're in the mid-court area and you have confidence in your lob, you should try for an offensive lob occasionally.

127

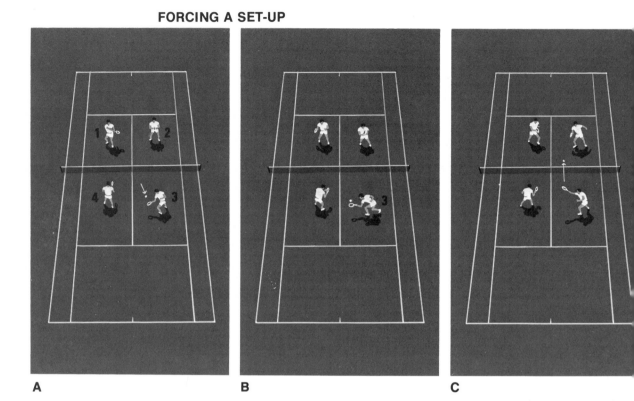

A   B   C

FORCING A SET-UP

Suppose we take that last situation a few steps further. Let's say the point has continued so that all four players are at the net and in good volleying positions. What is the tactic to use now?

As long as the ball is fairly high over the net the players will be able to volley easily, so the objective should be to get the ball low over the net and, preferably, toward the feet of one of the players who will be forced to hit up. Hitting a volley up has two disadvantages: hitting a low volley is harder than hitting a high volley; and after the stroke the ball will be rising over the net and so present a putaway situation for the other team.

Let's suppose that Player 1 hits a slice volley (Fig. A) with very little pace so that it drops sharply as it crosses the net toward the feet of Player 3 (B). Player 3 then has to bend

128

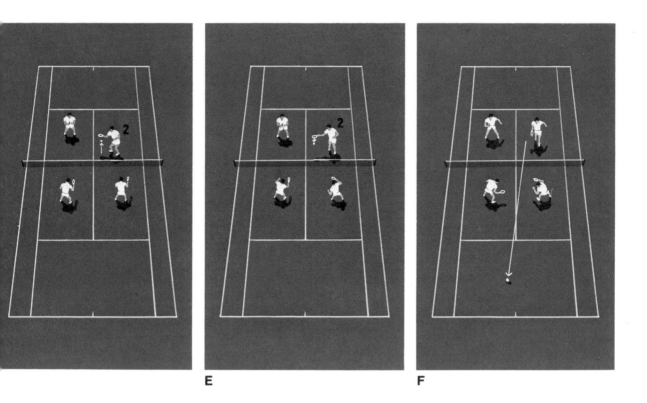

E

F

down and hit either a very low volley (C) or even a half volley if the ball bounces. If he hits a low volley he'll have to lift it over the net (D), but he can't afford to hit the ball too hard because that will make the ball rise high over the net.

By now, Player 2 will have realized that the ball will be rising as it crosses the net and so a set-up situation presents itself. He moves closer to the net (E) and hits a powerful volley between the two opposing players for a winner (F). Players 1 and 2 have demonstrated one of the keys to successful doubles: they have played as a team with one member setting up a situation and the other putting the ball away. In that respect, doubles is like chess—you set up the play and then move in for the kill.

They have also demonstrated an important factor in net play: always try to force your opponents to hit up. The objective is to make your opponents hit up so that you can then hit down.

THE POACH

A   B   C

THE POACH

The doubles tactics I have just described you will both use and encounter often—they are the basic plays in a doubles team's repertoire. The poach, on the other hand, is a tactic that should be used only occasionally as a surprise weapon. Poaching occurs when the net player moves over into the server's half of the court to volley away a crosscourt return of serve. It is, literally, poaching on the server's territory. Poaching should be used only when the poacher is confident that a winning volley can be made and only when both team members are aware that a poach is to be tried.

You and your partner should agree to poach, say, on the first point of the next game or to have signals—a closed fist behind the net player's back is sometimes used—to show that a poach is about to be tried.

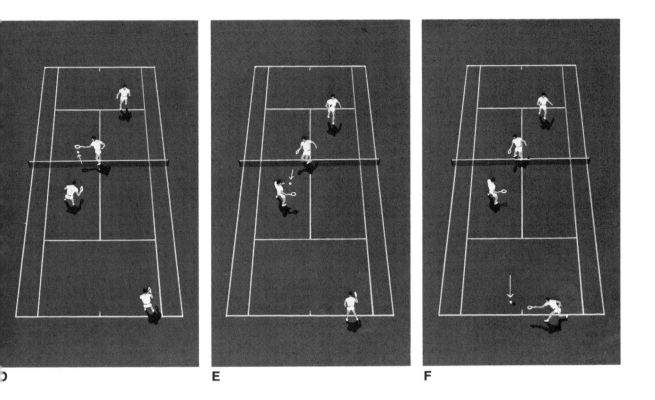

D   E   F

Poaching is a pretty simple maneuver, but it calls for some fast footwork and accurate volleying from the net player. Let's follow through the sequence of a poach. The server serves into the deuce court (Fig. A), and the receiver hits a cross-court return (B). As soon as the receiver hits the ball, the net player starts to dash over into the server's half of the court (C). At that point, the server, who was moving to the net, changes direction and moves over into the net player's court to cover that half in the case of unsuccessful volley by the poacher.

The net player then closes up on the return (D) and either volleys the ball directly at the opposing net player (E) or between the two opposing players (F). Either way, the volley should be a winner and the point will be concluded. Only one or two successful poaches are needed to confuse the opposition and put the receiver off his return.

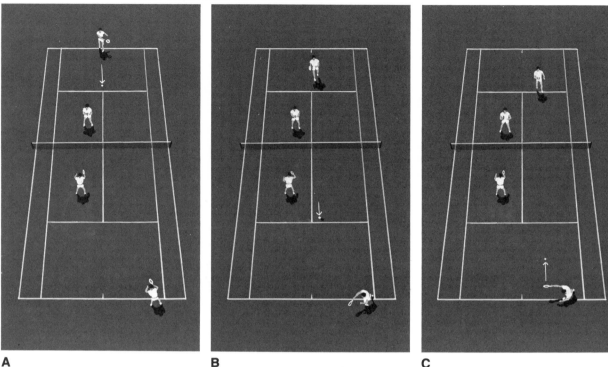

A   B   C

THE AUSTRALIAN FORMATION

Another occasional tactic you should try is the "Australian serving formation," in which the server and the net player both stand in the same half of the court. This is a very good tactic against a receiver with an excellent low crosscourt return of serve. Having the net player on the server's side to intercept the crosscourt return and volley it away, just as the poacher does, usually forces the receiver to go for the more difficult down-the-line return. So the Australian formation will have the effect of upsetting your opponents and may help to turn a losing game to your favor.

When using the Australian formation (Fig. A), the server stands close to the center mark ready to run into the other half of the court to take the expected down-the-line return. The net player stands in the usual volleying position, maybe a

132

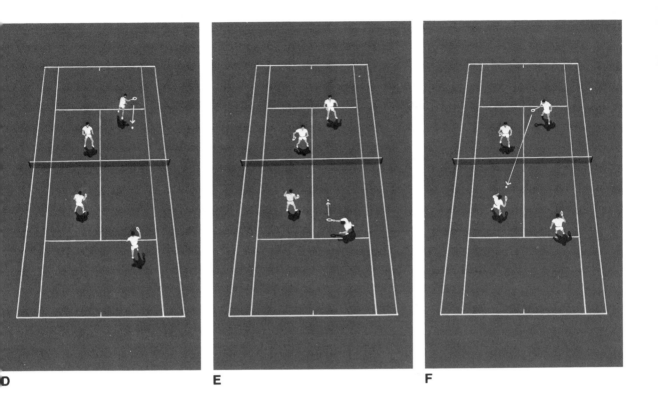

D   E   F

little closer to the center line than to the singles sideline. The server should serve down the middle of the court (B) so that the return (C) doesn't go directly back down the alley. If the serve is close to the center line, the return will, most likely, come in the middle of the left court so that the net-rushing server (D) can make a first volley toward the receiver (E). As an alternative, a high down-the-line return of serve might be volleyed at the opposing net player (F).

The Australian formation can also be used when serving into the ad court, where it is safe to serve wide to the backhand since an offensive down-the-line backhand return is very difficult to make. The oncoming server should be presented with a fairly easy forehand volley. Chances are, though, that you'll want to use the Australian formation only when you are serving into the deuce court and will revert to the conventional formation when serving into the ad court.

133

DOUBLES STRATEGY

MIXED DOUBLES

At the professional level, the game of mixed doubles doesn't get the attention it deserves. Yet some of the most entertaining tennis is played in the mixed doubles championships, as I found out for myself when I used to play—and win—mixed doubles with Gussie Moran. The intermediate player will learn more about tennis and see the strategies and tactics that are more appropriate to the average player's game by watching such mixed doubles teams as Margaret Court and Marty Riessen, or Owen Davidson and Billie Jean King, than by watching the top men's doubles teams. The pace of mixed doubles is slower and the shotmaking often more varied, with long rallies so that the spectators get their money's worth.

The general principles of mixed doubles play are no different from those of men's or women's doubles. The only differences come when there is a big gap between the skills of the two partners. In that case, the stronger player, whether male or female, will naturally take on more of the load of hitting the winning points, of retreating to hit overheads, of hitting the confusing volleys down the middle of the court, and so on. When I play with my wife I find myself taking more of the play just as, I'm sure, Billie Jean King will take most of the play when she is partnered by her husband Larry.

Playing with your spouse does call for more consideration than playing with any other partner. If you are the stronger player and take so many of the shots that you almost push your spouse off the court, I doubt that your tennis-playing partnership will last too long! If you're the weaker player you won't want the humiliation of taking only the very easy shots. The stronger partner should exercise some restraint in the interests of better tennis and a happier partnership.

When there is a sizable difference in ability, the weaker

player should normally play in the forehand court so that the stronger player can receive serve on the more critical advantage points. The weaker player should serve with the wind or, on a very sunny day, away from the sun, to gain maximum advantage from the elements. I'd also advise the weaker player to stand a little closer to the net where it's a bit easier to volley. You can agree beforehand that the better player will always move back to smash the lobs.

Most intermediate players play mixed doubles for social reasons—to have some enjoyable tennis that is not too arduous. If that is the case, then I think you should play your best game but try to keep the ball in play as long as possible. Resist the temptation to end the point by slamming the ball at the weaker player or by poaching on a relatively weak service return. Make the tennis fun for the other players and you'll enjoy it more yourself.

Of course, if you decide to play mixed doubles competitively, then your attitude to the weaker player will change. You should take advantage of that player's weakness just as if you were playing a men's or women's doubles match. You should serve to the other player's weakness and take advantage of the weaker serve to hit the ball early and go for winners on the return of serve. If you're playing with a weaker partner, you should be prepared to cover more of the court and to move back for the overheads. If you are the weaker partner, then concentrate on just getting the ball back over the net, and let your partner make most of the winning shots. If you both agree beforehand on your responsibilities and limitations there's no reason why competitive mixed doubles should not also be enjoyable mixed doubles.

DOUBLES STRATEGY

THE FOUR MOST COMMON DOUBLES ERRORS

The worst error you can possibly make in doubles is to try to do too much with the ball—going for low-percentage shots that end up as errors more than winners. Hit the shots that you know you can make and keep the ball in play. In most doubles matches, the number of errors far exceeds the number of winners, which means that points are won mostly on your opponents' errors. All you have to do is give them the opportunity to hang themselves and, chances are, they will.

At the intermediate level a second error often seen is a lack of communication between the two partners. Commonly, the net player poaches without informing his or her partner first so that there is complete confusion, especially if the poach is unsuccessful. At its worst, this lack of communication results in one player becoming more and more angry with the other to the point where their play is affected. If you can't communicate with your partner or your partner won't communicate with you, find another player who will. You can't play doubles unless you talk to each other.

The third most common error occurs when both players go for the ball together and clash rackets, often muffing the shot and losing the point. Before you start a match, agree that the stronger player will take most of the confusing shots—those that come down the middle of the court. If there is any doubt at all, the player who is nearest to the ball should shout "Mine!" or "Yours!" as loudly as possible. When I play with Hugh Stewart, my teaching professional at Caesars Palace, I often find that I'm faster at getting to a shot that, strictly speaking, should be his. So I yell at him and take the ball. Fortunately, we understand each other very well so Hugh doesn't get upset by this tactic—especially when we win. Which we do quite often!

Finally, the fourth most common error in doubles is not one of play but of strokemaking. Few intermediate players practice the overhead enough, so they tend to hit very poor smashes in competitive matches. A good doubles player must have an effective overhead because the opposition will inevitably resort to the lob from time to time. Although a lob will draw you away from the net, a good smash will help you keep the offensive and stop the other team from coming to the net immediately. If your overhead is weak, make sure that you include plenty of these strokes in your regular practice sessions.

9

TOURNAMENT PLAY

TOURNAMENT PLAY

TENNIS TOURNAMENTS

Playing in or helping with a tennis tournament are ways of increasing your enjoyment of the sport. Later in this chapter I'll be giving you advice on the most important activity at a tournament—winning—but for now I'd like to tell you about the different types of tournaments you can expect to encounter as a club player.

Most major tournaments are single elimination, with all the entries matched in the first round, the winner of each match advancing to the second round and the loser dropping from play. Each round eliminates half the players until only two are left to face each other in a final match. Just one loss will eliminate a player, so this tournament is most suited to large entry fields when only a short time is available for play.

If all the players are of equal ability, the names are placed in a hat and entered on the draw sheet in the order in which they are pulled out of the hat. In top-level tournaments, the best players are ranked in order of their recent playing records and entered or "seeded" in specific positions in the draw. This avoids having the two best players meet in the first or second round. In a seeded draw, the first seed is placed at the top of the upper half of the draw and the second seed at the bottom of the lower half. The other seeds are then placed proportionately throughout the draw.

In a single elimination draw where the number of players is not a multiple of two, i.e., 8, 16, 32, and so on, "byes" are entered so that a player with a bye advances directly into the second round. Byes are usually placed at the top and bottom of the draw.

Because the single elimination tournament drops half the players in the first round, many clubs run consolation tournaments for the first and sometimes the second round losers.

All the losing players are entered in another draw and compete for separate prizes from the main draw. A variation on the consolation tournament is the so-called windmill tournament, where a player moves to a separate consolation tournament each time after losing. Windmill tournaments are very difficult to organize but excellent for groups of varying ability, since each player will find his or her skill level after a couple of matches. Everyone entered will get to play several matches instead of being eliminated after only one or two.

Round-robin tournaments also give players the chance to play several matches. In a true round robin, every player plays every other player once and game scores are totaled to find the absolute winner. In round robins with many contestants, the participants are often divided into "flights" of no more than eight players to cut down on the number of matches that have to be played.

Change-up, change-down tournaments are great fun when there are many players of differing abilities. In this type of tournament, the courts are numbered and players arbitrarily assigned to a court. The winner of a match moves to the next lower numbered court and the loser moves to the next higher numbered court. To keep matches short, a time limit is often imposed on each match. After several rounds, the best players should end up facing each other on court 1. A variation on this tournament is to have doubles play where the teams change partners after changing courts. Games won are totaled for each player and the player with the highest number of victories at the end is the overall winner.

In all the tournaments I've just described you may find special tournaments for limited groups such as over-forty-five players, A, B or C (arbitrary tennis club class) players, juniors (eighteen or under), and so on. In doubles tournaments you'll find contests for family combinations such as husband and wife, father and son, or mother and daughter. Within a good

tennis club there will be a considerable variety of tournament play so you should always be able to find some competition that suits your game and is fun to play.

TOURNAMENT PREPARATION AND PLAY

Tennis is a competitive game and everyone who plays, of any age, likes the psychological satisfaction of winning. If you're like most players you'll soon be looking around for competition outside your immediate circle of tennis friends. When that happens I suggest you enter a local tournament. Pick one organized by your parks and recreation department, your local tennis association or your tennis club if you are a member. Almost all recreation departments and clubs run a wide variety of tournaments for all ages and abilities so you ought to be able to find one that won't leave you feeling outclassed. When you do enter a tournament, though, I think you ought to prepare and play in a thoroughly professional way. After all, you'd like to win, wouldn't you?

It almost goes without saying that you should be in good condition and your game should be well practiced in the weeks before a tournament. *If you are a senior player, remember you may have to play several really tough matches over a couple of days. If you have any doubts about standing up to that much exercise, consult your physician first.*

The day before a big tournament you should relax as much as possible. In fact, I wouldn't play much tennis that day—just take it easy so that you're relaxed and can get a good night's sleep before the big day. On the actual day, get up early and, if possible, go out on the court and practice for about a half hour to loosen up. Play gently at first, gradually working your game up to its peak. Play for about 10 minutes at a time and then rest a few minutes. Don't overextend yourself during this last practice session. After practice, shower, get into some dry clothes, and lie down until about an hour before you have to turn up for your match. Get a little sleep if you can and you'll feel completely refreshed.

I would not recommend eating or drinking much before a match. My breakfast before a big match would be some orange juice, a couple of soft-boiled eggs, and a slice of toast. Just before the match I'd sip some warm tea sweetened with honey. A big meal before a match will increase the chances of stomach cramps, especially for the older player. You don't need a heavy meal because your body will have plenty of stored energy to see you through the match. Before the match you'll be allowed 3 minutes to warm up. Do just that. Don't use the time to practice. Hit some nice flowing ground strokes and run around to limber up and loosen your leg muscles. Bend your knees a lot to help the leg muscles warm up.

Chances are you'll be nervous about the match and it will take you longer than usual to get into your normal game. Don't worry about that. Your opponent will be having exactly the same problems. Probably your opponent didn't sleep too well the night before either and will be just as badly off as you.

Unless you're very confident about your serve, I'd suggest you elect to receive serve if you win the toss. Just concentrate on getting the ball back over the net for the first few games and let your opponent make all the errors. The first server often makes many errors because of "first-game" jitters. When it's your turn to serve, concentrate on getting your serve in and hold back on doing much with it until you're a little more relaxed. Above all, don't show your opponent you're nervous by becoming exasperated with yourself or complaining about your inability to hit the ball. Disguise your discomfort and don't let your opponent feel there's a chance of getting the upper hand in the match.

You should always have some strategy mapped out before you start the match. For example, if you know your opponent has a weak forehand, play to it. Even if your opponent starts out hitting well with the forehand, your constant attack on that side will soon bring out the flaws in that shot—the more you punish a weak shot, the weaker it will get. On the other hand, avoid your opponent's strength. For example, whenever I played Ken Rosewall I avoided his backhand because I knew it would get better as the match progressed.

If the match tips in your favor, you'll become more relaxed as time goes by and the standard of your play should go up. But don't let your concentration drop just because you're one set ahead. Tennis is a game where success can ebb and flow very rapidly. If you lose your concentration for a couple of games, that can restore your opponent's concentration enough to turn your winning game into a losing game. Don't let up on your play until the final point is over, even if you're well ahead. I have seen many matches where a player has won after being a set down and 5–love in the second set.

If you're losing, don't give up. Your opponent's hot streak can be broken. You can change a losing game. In fact, the professional's advice is never change a winning game but always try to change a losing game. The first thing you can do is increase your concentration. Stare at the ball as though you expect it to disappear at any moment. Then try changing the tempo of the game. If you've been net rushing, stay back and play from the baseline. If you've been playing on the baseline, try going to net a few times. Slow down or speed up between serves. Vary your shots. Use more lobs or more short shots to get your opponent moving about the court. Above all: keep the opposition guessing about your intentions and you'll see your game begin to change.

After the match, congratulate your opponent or accept congratulations graciously, thank the umpire and the linesmen, and go get a shower right away. Don't hang around in wet clothes to watch the next match. *For the senior player it's doubly important to have a warm shower and stay bundled up until your body can adjust to the outside temperature.* This is especially vital if you're playing indoors during the winter months. If you expect to have to play again that day, lie down and get some sleep.

SELECTING EQUIPMENT

SELECTING A TENNIS RACKET

As a tennis player, the most important purchasing decision you'll make is the selection of your racket. Buying a tennis racket is like buying a new car—there's no substitute for the test run. Before you buy a new racket, test-play as many models as you can. Borrow rackets from friends; lean on your local sporting goods store or your club's pro shop; use every method to find a racket that suits your style of play.

I'm often asked if there are serious differences between wood, metal, and fiberglass rackets. The answer is that for the average player, there's little difference if rackets are of similar quality. A professional might notice that the ball will leave a metal racket a little faster and with slightly less control, but most average players would barely notice. *Players over forty may feel that a flexible wood racket will jar the arm less and ease any muscular problem such as tennis elbow.*

It is important to choose the correct weight and grip size and have the racket strung to the tension that best suits your game. A racket of the wrong size will feel uncomfortable; a tightly strung racket will make the balls bounce off the strings too fast; and a loosely strung racket will feel "dead" on impact and sap power from your shots.

Most men feel comfortable with an evenly balanced racket that weighs between 13 and 13½ ounces. Most women will find that rackets weighing between 12 and 12½ ounces suit them best. Personally, I like to use a heavy racket when I'm training for an important match, then switch to a 13-ounce racket for the match itself. The heavier racket helps strengthen my arm, but in the match I have to adjust to the lighter racket, which whips through the air faster and causes my shots to go deeper. Most players might not be able to adjust fast enough so I'd recommend they stick with the same weight for all practice and match play. *As you get older you'll probably find a lighter racket easier to swing.*

Grip size is just as important as weight. Many players use grip sizes so large the racket wobbles in their hands. It's tough to give a rule for measuring your grip because the geometry of the hand varies so much from person to person. But there's no substitute for testing a few grip sizes. Remember to grip the racket properly (see page 11) when checking grip sizes.

Most men find a comfortable grip size between 4½ and 4¾ inches; women usually prefer a grip of 4¼ to 4½ inches. If the grip is too big the racket will twist in your hand as you play; you can guard against that before you buy your racket by asking someone to twist it when you are gripping it normally. If the racket is too small, the skin of your palm and fingers will wrinkle and cause blisters during a long match. If you have doubts about selecting the right grip size, check with your local pro.

It's best to buy a racket unstrung and have it strung to the tension you prefer. Unless you're a very serious tournament player, you should have your racket strung with a good-quality nylon string. The advantages of gut are not worth the much higher cost for the average player. Nylon not only costs less; it will also last longer and be less susceptible to damage from the elements and from grit picked up off the court.

String tension is largely a personal matter, but most players find a tension between 55 and 60 pounds satisfactory. It is worth experimenting with different tensions until you find the one that fits your game or playing situation. Don't go for very tight stringing if you suffer from tennis elbow. In areas where the air is thin, like Denver, your racket should be strung more loosely because the ball will be softer and would be squashed if hit hard by a tightly strung racket. *Players over forty may find a more loosely strung racket will help their game.* If you

have any doubts about the right tension for your area, seek the advice of a well-qualified tennis pro who knows your game and the courts where you play.

For long and faithful service you should take good care of your racket. Store it away from direct sunlight by hanging it in a rack or from a peg. Use a cover to protect the racket when not in use. A press is not really necessary for modern wood rackets but it won't do any harm. Keep the frame clean by swabbing it with a lint-free cloth soaked in alcohol, and clean the grip regularly with cold water.

From time to time you should renew the grip. Leather grips compress with use so that the racket may in time feel smaller in your hand. The grip will also become slick with heavy use, making it slippery. I change my grips about once a month, but you'll probably find about once every two or three months enough. The soft leather will give you a firm grip and feel comfortable. New grips cost only a few dollars and you can rewind the grip yourself with a little practice. A fresh leather grip can make an old racket feel like new again.

BUYING TENNIS BALLS

In medieval times, tennis balls were made from heavy felt stuffed with human hair. Even today the manufacture of tennis balls remains more an art than a science.

Almost all the tennis balls available in the United States are approved by the U.S. Tennis Association as conforming to the specifications of the International Lawn Tennis Federation. Unfortunately, the ILTF specifies size, weight, deformation, and bounce when the ball is new. There are no standards for durability of the ball. You may well find that three balls from the same can have different playing characteristics. I can only suggest you buy balls from a reputable store or pro shop, and, if they are very soft or totally dead the first time you use them, return them to the shop for replacement.

Balls come in a regular grade for play on smooth courts and a heavy-duty grade for play on abrasive surfaces. The heavy-duty balls have a tougher covering and tend to keep their "nap," or fuzz, longer when used on concrete. Both grades are pressurized in production and sold in a pressurized can so they won't go soft before purchase. In play all tennis balls will lose their pressure, becoming soft and eventually unplayable. How fast this deterioration occurs will depend on your style of play and the court surface, but I think it's well worthwhile to open a new can of balls every time you go out to play, if you can afford to.

In some parts of the country you can buy low-pressure tennis balls designed for high-altitude play where a standard ball would have too much bounce. If you live in a place as high as Denver, you ought to try high-altitude balls.

A few European suppliers offer "pressureless" balls that rely on a thicker rubber wall to produce the bounce. These balls are usually supplied in a box instead of a pressurized can. It is claimed that they have a longer life than pressurized balls, but many U.S. players find the pressureless balls heavy and more difficult to play.

Tennis balls now come in a variety of colors. The white tennis ball has almost disappeared in favor of the yellow ball, which is easier to see indoors or in poor light conditions outside. Other colors may look pretty but they serve no useful purpose.

SELECTING EQUIPMENT

BUYING TENNIS CLOTHES

Shoes are the most important item in your tennis wardrobe. A badly fitting pair of shoes will cause blisters and interfere with your concentration. Select tennis shoes on the basis of comfort, not appearance. I now buy my tennis shoes for comfort, although when I was playing as a professional, I often wore the lightest shoe I could find and put up with the discomfort. In those days it was important to have light shoes so that my footwork could be as fast as possible. If you value your feet, though, don't follow that example.

When you shop for tennis shoes, wear the type of socks you normally wear on the court. The shoe should have a substantial sole, especially if you play on the hard cement courts we have on the West Coast. For clay surfaces, choose the grooved soles that will help you get the sliding action vital to clay court play.

The upper parts of a tennis shoe may be canvas or leather. If the shoe is well made, the choice of upper is not so important. Leather shoes are more expensive and generally last longer, although the sole may wear out before the upper. If you are heavy on the soles of your shoes, a less expensive canvas shoe may be a smarter choice than a leather shoe. You'll have to experiment a little to find the best buy for you.

As an older player you may have problems with blisters on your feet. If so, you might try putting a thin foam insole inside your shoes. I have even used a foam insole inside my socks for extra comfort. If you do that, be careful when your remove the insoles—they have a tendency to stick to your feet and you can pull some skin off with the insole. Some players recommend wearing two pairs of socks but I've never found that very helpful.

BUYING TENNIS CLOTHES

You can play tennis in a wide variety of clothes—take a look at almost any public parks courts and you'll see what I mean. But I feel that the serious player will perform better dressed in clothes specifically designed for tennis.

If you can afford them, buy top-quality tennis clothes—they will fit better, launder more easily, and last longer. When you buy tennis clothes, be sure you have plenty of freedom of movement for your arms and legs. Cotton or cotton/polyester mixtures are preferable to all-synthetic fabrics because the cotton helps absorb perspiration and makes you feel cooler.

Older players especially should buy tennis jackets or warm-up suits to help their muscles warm up quickly and to prevent their bodies from cooling off too quickly after a match. As you get older it becomes more important that you treat your body carefully to prevent muscle problems and to avoid chills.

You'll find that sweatbands for your head and wrist are very helpful in absorbing perspiration. I keep several wristbands in my tennis bag and change them as often as necessary to stop the sweat from running onto my grip.

If you play in a very sunny climate you may find a hat helpful, although I've always found them a nuisance because the brim seems to interfere with my vision. Of course, if you have sensitive skin, like Rod Laver, then a hat becomes essential and you'll probably get used to using it. When my hair was quite long I did wear a hat to keep the hair out of my eyes, but I solved that problem by cutting my hair shorter. This sort of solution is up to you. It all depends how keen you are on the game.

PLAYING BETTER TENNIS

PLAYING BETTER TENNIS

laying good tennis is mainly a matter of having a well-grooved stroke arsenal and a thorough knowledge of the tactics and strategies of the doubles and singles games. And, of course, you must know how to combine these elements. But there are other factors to consider that influence your tennis game: tennis lessons; conditioning; tennis ailments; court surfaces; and the effects of wind and sun on your game.

TAKING TENNIS LESSONS

Whether you're a beginner or a good player with years of experience, you can benefit by taking lessons from a skilled tennis instructor. As a beginner, it's important that you start tennis play with some understanding of the correct stroke-making. As a more advanced player, you should be aware of the bad habits that inevitably creep into your game. In both cases, lessons with a good teaching pro will be money well spent.

If you are a beginner, I'd suggest you try group lessons first. Many public parks departments run quite good, inexpensive group programs during the tennis season. If you live in a part of the country with indoor tennis clubs, you might want to try a beginner's clinic in the winter so you'll be in good shape to play outdoors in the summer. Indoor tennis clinics are more expensive than the public parks programs, but the groups are often smaller so you may get more individual attention. In addition to the instruction, you'll also meet other players on your level with whom you can practice when the teaching sessions are over. If you do take a group lesson, it's important to practice what you've learned immediately after the lesson and daily thereafter, if you can, until you take the next lesson.

Since group lessons often have several instructors, you'll soon see the very great differences in ability among teaching professionals. If you're lucky, you may find one teacher who will be able to give you private lessons after you are past the beginner's stage. For anyone who can hit a ball adequately and has a year or two of playing experience, I'd recommend you take lessons privately or with a group of only two or three friends. The analysis of tennis stroking and playing calls for very close attention on the part of a teaching pro and that can be done best in private lessons.

Your major problem will be finding a teaching professional with the skills and personality you'll need to improve your game. Finding a good tennis pro is as hard as finding a good auto mechanic. Ask all the players you know for their recommendations. When you have a short list of pros, go to their clubs and ask if you can watch a lesson in progress. Ask the students for their reactions to the pro's teaching. Finally, take a trial lesson to see if the pro can improve your game. If you find a pro you like, stay put and take lessons at regular intervals. Each pro will have a different style of teaching. If you switch around, your game will inevitably suffer.

For the over-forty player I'd suggest you take lessons from a good local teaching pro who will be able to handle your development from a beginner up to a good local tournament player in your age group. It is not necessary to take lessons from a "name" tennis player like Pancho Segura or myself. When I give a lesson, I usually do so for an advanced or professional player like Roscoe Tanner or Vijay Amritraj. That lesson is usually 1 hour of concentrated stroke correction followed by at least 3 hours of grueling practice to get the lesson really grooved. The average player wouldn't be able to stand such a program.

Of course, if you find you're becoming an exceptional player, you will have to upgrade the level of your lessons. Your teaching pro should be honest enough to tell you when he can't take you any further and he should be able to recommend someone who can teach you at a higher level.

You can also get quite good instruction at some of the weekend or week-long tennis clinics offered at schools and resorts around the country. But I think you might see more improvement from spending the same amount of money on private lessons spread out over a period of several weeks. You won't retain everything you're taught in one week of concentrated instruction and you won't have enough time—or energy—to practice sufficiently to groove the stroke improvements that the clinic offers.

KEEPING IN CONDITION FOR TENNIS

If you intend to play tennis to win, you must be in good physical condition. Not only will you feel better if you're in top physical shape, but you'll enjoy your matches more and you'll be able to play more tennis without suffering from exhaustion or muscular ailments. *If you are an older person just beginning tennis or if you have had a long layoff because of illness, you must get a thorough checkup from your physician.* Explain that you want to take up tennis and ask your physician for recommendations on a training program to get you in shape and keep you there.

It isn't enough to just play tennis every day to keep in shape for playing tennis. Even the professional tennis players who play several hours a day undergo physical training programs involving sprinting, exercising, and stamina conditioning. If you want to put the most into your tennis and get the maximum enjoyment out of it at the same time, I suggest you have a regular conditioning program in addition to frequent tennis play.

While you should rely mainly on the advice of your physician, I think a training program for the older player should include:

Running—plain jogging will improve your stamina and increase the capacity of your heart and lungs.

Jumping rope—a few minutes each day will improve your footwork tremendously.

Wind sprints—a series of short sprints, each about the length of a tennis court, will help both your footwork and your stamina.

Stationary exercises—toe-touching will strengthen your stomach muscles.

Arm and wrist exercises—squeezing an old tennis ball repeatedly in your hand plus a few simple dumbbell exercises will strengthen your arm and wrist muscles.

TENNIS AILMENTS

If you keep yourself in good condition and know your own physical limits, there's no reason why you should have to suffer to play tennis. Some players injure themselves by playing too hard before their muscles are warmed up or by playing for too long on a hot and humid day. *For the older player it's especially important that you recognize there are limits to your stamina.* After all, one of the objectives of weekend tennis players is to play to improve their physical health, not to damage it.

Nevertheless, you'll probably strain or pull a muscle at some point in your tennis career. As a professional I have played matches with muscle strains because I had an obligation not to disappoint the paying customers. The weekend player does not have that obligation. If you injure a muscle, get off the court and don't play until the muscle recovers. Whirlpool baths can be quite good for relaxing a sprained muscle. If the sprain is inflamed, ice may also soothe the inflammation. If the inflammation persists, then you should see your doctor.

The most common complaint among tennis players is, of course, tennis elbow—an inflammation of the tendons surrounding the elbow joint. *Tennis elbow can be very painful and is common among players over thirty-five. It is usually caused by faulty stroking—slapping at the ball, for example, on the backhand.* Most cases of tennis elbow will disappear as mysteriously as they came, often within a few months. Others may need medical treatment and a very few cases may need surgery. If you suffer from tennis elbow, it's unlikely you'll have to give up tennis. Try heat treatment before you play. If your elbow is still painful, it's important to play within your capabilities, stroking the ball in a way that causes as little pain as possible. Seek the advice of your pro, who may be able to spot the flaws in your stroking that caused tennis elbow. After getting tennis elbow, many players unconsciously change their strokes so the strain on the tendons is not aggravated and eventually the pain goes away. Some players have found that a brace around the fleshy part of the forearm lets them keep playing with tennis elbow. When I had tennis elbow several years ago, I found an electric heating pad effective before and after a match. Hot towels can also be helpful. You will have to experiment somewhat to find the solution to your own tennis elbow problem.

If you play tennis often you may get blisters and wrinkled or cracked skin on the palm of your racket hand. I find that my hand becomes very dry from handling the leather grip, so I use lots of baby lotion after a match to keep my skin lubricated and flexible. I think I have a bottle of baby lotion in almost every room of the house so I can put some on whenever I have a spare minute. You can also tape your fingers at the points where the skin is likely to crack. Put the tape on before your skin actually cracks because it will be too painful after cracking.

As an older player, you should beware of the effects of heat exhaustion. Take salt tablets on hot days before you play and drink liquids throughout the match so you don't become dehydrated. If you're playing on a very hot day and your eyesight begins to go fuzzy or you get a headache, then the time has come to stop playing, get a change of clothes, lie down, and rest for a while. If a player collapses from the heat, then immediate medical attention is advisable. Better that you stop playing before things get to that stage.

When you have finished playing, make it a point to take a shower and change into dry clothes. Following the shower, stay warm and bundled up until your body adjusts to the room temperature. If you can't take a shower, at least change out of your wet clothes. After playing a strenuous match I like to lie down and sleep for a while. Sleep is a great way of letting your body recuperate after physical activity. Having benefited from an hour's sleep you'll be ready to play again or to continue with other activities.

TENNIS COURT SURFACES

During the last few years there has been a real boom in the variety of tennis surfaces. It seems that everyone is trying to produce an "ideal" tennis court surface. Fortunately or otherwise, it's just not possible to produce a surface that will satisfy all players—beginners prefer slow-playing courts while the top pros like faster courts that favor the serve and volley game. So you'll probably encounter a variety of tennis court surfaces, especially if you play outdoors in the summer, indoors in the winter, and in other parts of the country on your vacations. If you have some basic knowledge of the types of surfaces around, you'll be able to adjust your tennis game accordingly.

The surfaces you'll probably play on are composition or clay-type courts, hard courts of the asphalt or cement variety, cushioned courts laid on top of concrete or asphalt, grass courts, and the artificial, mostly indoor surfaces.

In the Northeast and Florida, clay-type courts predominate. The clay courts have a loose, gritty surface that slows the ball down and makes it bounce relatively high. Clay courts favor the beginner since the pace of play is slow and the rallies can be long. Clay court players usually adopt a baseline style of play and go to the net only when they're sure of winning the point. *The surface is easy on the feet since you can slide to a stop without jarring your legs. Many older players like this feature of clay-type courts.* I find the pace of play too slow on clay-type courts and the footing too loose for the rapid footwork essential to my serve and volley game.

In the West, cement courts dominate. I learned to play on concrete and believe that surface to be the supreme test of a top tennis player's ability. The ball stays low and the bounce is fast, so concrete favors the players with a big serve and a net-

162

rushing game. Asphalt is similar in performance to concrete, but a little slower, especially when the surface gets hot and begins to soften a little. Both types of court can be very hard on the feet. *To avoid jarring your leg muscles, you must learn to bend your knees to cushion the shock as you run around the court and stop quickly to hit the ball.*

For the older player, a compromise between the slow composition surfaces and the fast hard courts is the cushioned court, where a layer of resilient material is poured on top of an asphalt or concrete court. Cushioned courts are very comfortable on the feet and can be built to be fairly slow or very fast. The bounce is often high and uniform, as long as the court is well constructed. However, cushioned courts are expensive to install and are prone to damage if subjected to non-tennis-playing traffic. Consequently, you're likely to find cushioned courts only at the better tennis clubs or indoor tennis centers.

Grass is, of course, the original surface for what used to be called "lawn" tennis, but such courts are awfully expensive to maintain and can be used for only a few months of the year. Grass courts are gradually disappearing from the tennis scene; if you can manage to play on one before they finally disappear, do so. Grass is a wonderfully soft surface like an expensive carpet. A hard-hit ball will skid on grass and stay low, so the surface favors the serve and volley player who can hit a return of serve before it bounces. The bounce is notoriously uneven on most grass courts—another reason for taking the ball before it bounces.

THE EFFECTS OF WIND AND SUN

Tennis players are very fond of blaming their losses on outside factors that have nothing to do with their tennis-playing abilities. When a player loses, you'll often hear the loss blamed on equipment or the elements. Granted, wind and sun can have a damaging effect on your normal game, but they will affect your opponent's as well. Rather than using the elements as scapegoats, you should learn how to counter the effects of wind and sun and, maybe, put them to work for you in your game.

Wind is the most frustrating factor for an outdoor tennis player. At Caesars Palace in Las Vegas, where I'm director of tennis, desert winds sometimes come rushing in and make play almost impossible despite the wind screens that surround each court. Partly for that reason, even in sunny Nevada, we also have indoor courts.

When you are playing into a wind you can afford to hit a little harder than usual. On the other hand, when you are playing with the wind behind you, hit the ball a little softer so that the wind won't carry the ball beyond the opposing baseline. If you can hit a topspin shot, you can help the ball stay in court when the wind is behind you by adding extra topspin. The topspin will bring the ball down faster in the other court.

Serving becomes a real problem in a gusty wind, not only because the wind may blow your serve wide of the service box, but also because the wind may shift your service toss, making you mis-hit the serve. Tossing the ball lower will give the wind less time to affect your toss, and using spin will help pull the ball down into the service box.

One shot to avoid hitting in the wind is the high lob. Hitting a high lob in the wind is asking for trouble, especially if you hit it with the wind behind you. Chances are the wind will blow the lob behind the baseline and you'll lose the point. On the other hand, an offensive lob into the wind can be very effective because the wind will most likely keep the ball in court no matter how hard you hit it.

The sun can also affect your game, especially if you're playing in the late afternoon. Many tennis courts are laid out in a roughly north and south direction so that the effects of the sun are minimized for both players. But there will be times when you'll be serving and forced to look up at a ball that disappears because the sun is in your eyes. To keep yourself from being blinded, you can either try moving your serving position a little to one side or tossing the ball up to one side of its usual path. I prefer to move a little, since changing my toss can alter my service timing.

I don't think that sunglasses are much help. The glasses produce distracting reflections and they cut down on your visual sharpness, especially in the afternoon hours. I understand, though, that some contact lens wearers find sunglasses useful.

Because you change sides after every odd-numbered game, the effect of the sun will be nearly the same for both players, although it often seems that a convenient cloud appears just when your opponent is about to serve. You can, of course, make the sun work for you by lobbing into it so that your opponent has to hit an overhead with the sun in his eyes. But that's a pretty low trick, and you'll be asking for him to give you the same treatment when you change sides.

HOW TO PRACTICE

No one can expect to become a good tennis player without lots of practice. There simply is no substitute for practicing your entire arsenal of shots. If you want to improve your forehand, go out and hit forehands for 15 minutes every day. You may not see much improvement after a week but your opponents will know the difference after you've had a few weeks of steady practice. Even the great champions practice their strokes on an almost daily basis—that's how they got to be champions and that's how you stay at the top in professional tennis. It's just as true, however, for the average player. If you do not practice, you will lose the skills and your reflexes will slow down. *This is especially important for the older player who may not have had the various strokes grooved as a youngster. When you're young you have all the time in the world; when you get to be a little older it's tough to find the time for practice, but if you can, it will help your game.*

These days, it's also hard to find a court to practice on. Tennis is so popular that the courts are always booked and, especially if you're playing on an expensive indoor court, no one likes to think of "wasting" valuable court time on practice. Well, practice time is not "wasted" time. A few minutes of practice every time you go out to play will add greatly to the standard of your play and to your enjoyment of the game. *So, even if you can afford only one hour of tennis a week, plan to spend at least a quarter of that time practicing at least one stroke each time you play.*

Of course, you don't always need to have a court to practice, although I believe the best practice is done with a real partner in conditions as close as possible to a real tennis match. If you have a paved area in your back yard or an asphalt driveway, you can easily set up a backboard of thick plywood, or a commercially made rebound net, so that you can practice by yourself. And, in fact, to practice what is perhaps the most important shot in tennis, the serve, all you need is some space and a bucket of balls. You can easily set up targets and practice the motion and direction of your serve.

Although a backboard or rebound net is much better than no practice at all, such devices have their limitations. Every shot you hit against a backboard tends to come back the same way so that you soon get the feeling of grooving your shots, but you're making the same shot each time. In a real game you will be moving around the court since it's very unlikely that your opponent will put two balls in the same place in quick succession. So I'd suggest you angle your shots against the backboard, which will force you to run for each shot. That way not only will you be working on your stroking but your footwork should also improve.

However, there is a limit to the amount of practice anyone should take with a backboard. Working out against a backboard is very tiring and can be quite boring. So I'd suggest you play regular practice sessions with a friend. Agree to meet at least twice a week to practice your strokes against each other for, say, half an hour, followed by an hour of serious match play. Make a conscious effort to use your newly practiced strokes in the following sets.

There are any number of routines you can use to make your practice more exciting. I'll suggest a few that you can use as the basis of your own practice sessions, but you'll probably develop routines of your own depending on your own ability and needs.

Begin your practice sessions by hitting some easy forehands and backhands to each other to get your arm and leg muscles warmed up. I think this is very important for the older player who may not have many opportunities to exercise other than in regular tennis games. Run around and try to break a sweat before you start hitting out and running for those hard-to-get shots. When you are properly warmed up, start by hit-

ting forehands crosscourt to each other. If your shots are dropping far short of the baseline, add a little more height and power to your strokes until your shots land within about 3 feet of the baseline.

When you are getting the proper depth, return to the center of the baseline after each shot so that you have to run for each ball. Ground stroke practice should always include running for the ball since footwork is such an important part of tennis.

After a few minutes of crosscourt forehands, start hitting the ball down the line to your practice partner's backhand. Your practice partner should return the backhands down the line to your forehand. After a little while you can reverse the situation by moving to the other side of the court so that you can then hit backhands to your partner's forehand. Finally, of course, you should hit backhands crosscourt to each other. You can play almost endless variations on this theme. You can even give the practice a competitive edge by scoring points as you net the ball or hit it out of court. Naturally, the person with the largest number of points is the loser—the one who really needs the practice.

You'll probably find that about 15 minutes of concentrated ground stroke practice is as much as you can stand. Running around the court continuously is tiring, although it does have the additional side effect of helping to build up your stamina. When you've had enough ground stroke practice, go to the net and practice what I call "dink" tennis. A dink shot is a conventional ground stroke hit very gently so that the ball drops sharply in your opponent's court. Each of you should stand within a service court and hit volleys, dink shots, and drop shots to each other as though the lines of the service box constituted a miniature tennis court. Serve underhand and either see how long you can keep a rally going or score the game as though you were playing real tennis. "Dink" tennis is great for improving your control of the ball and for speeding up your reflexes at the net. It's also a lot of fun.

If you're lucky enough to have more than one practice partner, you can further improve your net play by using a two-on-one routine. In this game, two players stand up at the net in the usual volleying position for doubles while the third player stands near the baseline. The net players hit volleys to the baseline player, who tries to return every shot. It's a really grueling routine for the baseline player, who has to cover twice as much court as in conventional doubles. However, the net players shouldn't attempt to beat the baseliner—just keep the ball in play so that you develop steady, deep volleys that will be useful when you are playing real doubles. After 5 minutes of this drill, the baseliner should switch places with one of the net players. Keep rotating the positions for as long as you can stand the pace.

You can practice the serve either by yourself or with your practice partner. If you are by yourself and can get on a court, take a bucket of balls and aim your serves at tennis ball cans placed in the corners of the service court. Don't attempt to hit the ball hard until your shoulder and arm muscles are properly warmed up. Each time you practice the serve, hold two balls in your hand and imagine you are hitting a first serve followed by a second serve. Keep a note of the percentages you get in and check to see if there is an improvement week by week.

If you're practicing the serve with a partner, let the other player work on the service return as you work on your serve. After you have hit twenty or thirty serves, switch and practice your own service return. If you are an aggressive player, I'd suggest you also practice following your serve to the net and trying to volley the ball before it bounces. Practice sessions allow you to experiment with your serve and volley techniques. By practicing you'll be developing confidence in, say,

HOW TO PRACTICE

your twist serve or your ability to get to the net after the serve.

Finally, after the practice session you should play at least a couple of sets trying to put the practiced strokes into use. Play to win, of course, but let the experimentation that you used in your stroke practice carry over into your playing practice. That way you'll improve not only your strokes but your match play as well.

I think it is entirely appropriate that we complete this book with a chapter on practice. Not that the earlier chapters on stroking and strategy are any less important, of course. However, if you wish to play tennis well, and I assume that you do, you must take the time to practice. I cannot count the hours I used to spend, and still do spend, out on the court perfecting my strokes and refining the strategies I would later use in a match. Whether you are a beginner or a tournament player, practice is an essential part of your tennis play.

So I'd like to end the text of this book with a hope that uppermost among the ideas you have learned is the need for frequent practice. And practice your best strokes, too. It's been said that I had one of the most formidable serves ever seen on the tennis court. My serve developed that way because I knew it was one of my strengths and I have always followed the principle of improving on my best strokes although, of course, I certainly don't believe you should ignore your weaknesses. Never neglect your strengths and you'll find they will stay with you for a lifetime.

Now, go out, practice, play tennis and, above all, enjoy the sport.

APPENDIX:

HOW TO SCORE A MATCH

Tennis scoring has always seemed rather mysterious to non-tennis players. Terms like "love," "deuce," and "advantage" give tennis scoring a jargon of its own which all novice players have to struggle at first to learn. Tennis scoring is based more on tradition—being a holdover from the ancient game of court tennis—than on mathematics. Now that tennis has become such a popular sport there are moves to simplify the scoring. Simplified scoring would not only improve the scorekeeping problem but also make the game easier to understand for the TV sports fan. But for the time being at least, you'll have to master the traditional scoring system. Here's as simple a description as I can manage:

Tennis is scored by the point, game, set, and match. The first player to win six games or more with a lead of at least two games over the opponent wins a set. The first player to win two sets wins the match (called a "best-of-three" sets match), except in some men's tournament matches where the first player to win three sets wins the match (called a "best-of-five" sets match).

In scoring a game, the first player to win a point is said to have scored 15. If that player wins a second point, his score is 30. After winning the third point, his score is 40, and if he wins the next point he's won the game. However, when both players have won three points (40–40), the score is called "deuce." The next point is called "advantage." If the winner of the advantage point then wins the next point, that player wins the game. If not, the score reverts to deuce and the game continues until one player wins the two points immediately following a score at deuce.

It's a nice courtesy for the server to announce the score before serving, declaring his own score first. For example, a server winning the first point should announce "15–love." Love means a score of zero. If the server were to lose the first point, the score would be "love–15." If the score is even—such as 30–30—the server should announce "30–all." When the score is tied at 40–40, the call is "deuce." If the server scores the advantage point, the call will be "advantage-in," usually shortened to "ad-in." If the receiver scores the advantage point, the call will be "ad-out."

Since a set must be won by a margin of at least two games, sets can go on forever. For example, one of the longest matches on record was played at the U.S. Indoor Championships at Salisbury, Maryland, in 1968, between Mark Cox and Robert Wilson of Britain and Ron Holmberg and Charlie Pasarell of the United States. The score was 26–24, 17–19, 30–28, and the match lasted for over 6 hours.

To stop such marathon duels, almost all tournaments now use a tiebreaker game when the score reaches 6–all in games. However, there are several tiebreakers and their use can get very complicated, especially if you're playing in a doubles match.

Probably the simplest tiebreaker is the 9-point "sudden death" method. Here the set is decided by a best-of-9-points game after a game score of 6–all. The first player or team to score 5 points wins the tiebreaker and the set. Since, at 4–all, a single point can decide the set, this tiebreaker has been called "sudden death." It is very popular with the tennis fans, but the professionals don't like the outcome of a set or even of a match to be decided on a single point.

In a singles tiebreaker, the player who would ordinarily serve the next game serves the first 2 points of the tiebreaker. Then the opponent serves 2 points. The players then change sides and each serves 2 more points (if necessary). If the score reaches 4–all, the player who served last serves the last point and the opponent can choose to receive in either the ad or the deuce court.

In a doubles tiebreaker, the team that would have served

next begins to serve the first 2 points of the tiebreaker. Either player of the team can decide to serve first. After 2 points the serve changes to the other team, which then serves 2 points with its own choice of first server. The teams then change sides and the other partners serve 2 points each. If a deciding point is necessary, the player who served last serves the final point and the other team can choose the court in which it wishes to receive serve.

The professionals and the International Lawn Tennis Federation are not in favor of the 9-point tiebreaker and have authorized a 12-point system, sometimes called "lingering death" by its opponents because the winner must have a 2-point advantage to win. So the winner of a 12-point tiebreaker must win at least 7 points, with a 2-point lead over the opposing player. In theory, at least, a 12-point tiebreaker could go on indefinitely—hence "lingering death." In the 12-point tiebreaker the players alternate serves after each odd-numbered point.

The tiebreaker system is largely the brainchild of a Newport, Rhode Island, millionaire and tennis patron, James H. Van Alen. Jimmy Van Alen has also developed a completely new scoring system called the Van Alen Simplified Scoring System, or VASSS for short. VASSS games are scored 1–2–3–4 and the first player to win 4 points wins the game. There is a maximum of 7 points in a game. The advantage point is eliminated completely so the system is sometimes called "no-ad." At 3-points-all the receiver has a choice of side to make a return. If the game score is tied at 5–all, a 9-point tiebreaker is used to determine the set. This method of scoring has been used very successfully in some USTA tournaments and in several college tennis tournaments.

Van Alen has also proposed a set scoring system based on table tennis scoring, but that system has not yet met with much approval.

INDEX

INDEX

179

INDEX